T0190908

To:

....

From:

....

Date:

....

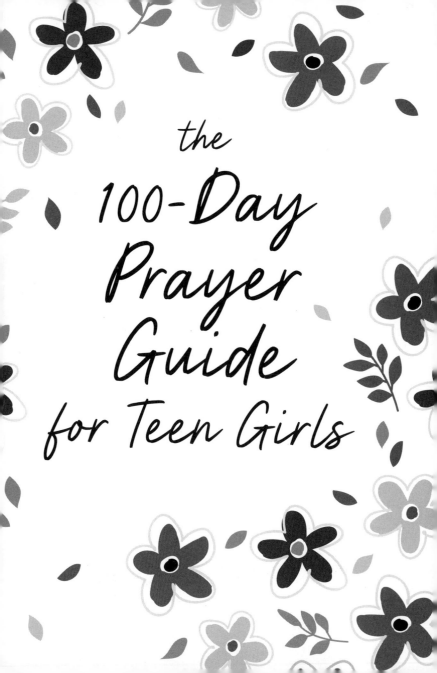

the

100-Day

Prayer

Guide

for Teen Girls

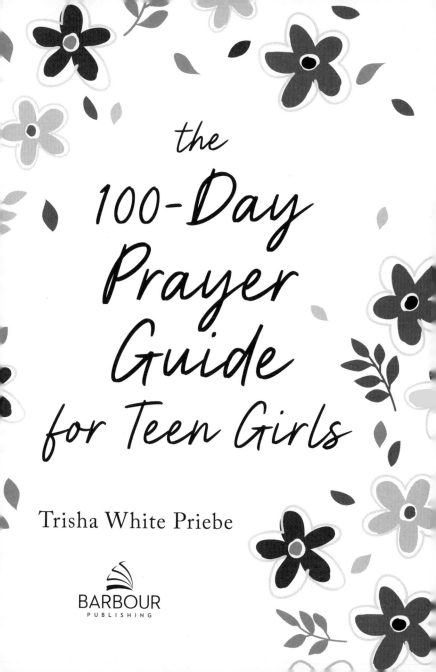

the

100-Day
Prayer
Guide
for Teen Girls

Trisha White Priebe

BARBOUR
PUBLISHING

*With a heart full of gratitude, to Sonja.
I'm thankful your faith has been made sight,
but I miss you every day.*

ISBN 978-1-63609-942-2

Published by Barbour Publishing, Inc., 1810 Barbour Drive, Uhrichsville, Ohio 44683, www.barbourbooks.com

Our mission is to inspire the world with the life-changing message of the Bible.

Member of the
Evangelical Christian
Publishers Association

Printed in China.

Get on the Road to a More Powerful Prayer Life

The 100-Day Prayer Guide for Teen Girls offers relatable, real-life wisdom and inspiration for prayer. You'll encounter page after page of biblical truths you can apply to your own quiet time with God.

It covers overarching topics like praise, confession, and intercession, as well as more specific issues, such as

- family
- culture
- the lost
- healing
- physical needs
- and much more.

This book provides a scripture on each subject, a helpful devotional thought, guidance on incorporating the topic into your own prayer life, and a short prayer starter.

It's a perfect way to spend your next hundred days!

1.
As Important as the Air We Breathe

I love the Lord, because He
hears my voice and my prayers.
Psalm 116:1

God has chosen prayer to be a way we receive His help in our lives. Just like we need air to breathe, we can't truly live without prayer. Prayer is the oxygen of the Christian life.

Our road map for this book is simple. In the next hundred days, we'll learn as much as we possibly can about this good gift God has given us.

Together, we'll explore different kinds of prayer, from quiet moments of reflection to urgent cries for help. We'll answer questions like "What does it mean to 'pray without ceasing'?" or "When should I stop praying for something?" We'll learn to listen, to speak, to sit in silence, and to pour our hearts out before Him.

In the coming days, we'll cross paths many times with David, since he had much to say about prayer in his writing of scripture. Today, let's simply consider his words in Psalm 116:1—

"I love the Lord, because He hears my voice and my prayers."

The same God who spoke the world into existence wants to hear what *you* have to say to Him. Isn't that incredible? Like it was for David, this is worthy of our love.

Think About It

- On a scale of 1 to 10, how much do you enjoy prayer? Why?

- When was the last time you prayed to God about something really important?

- What could you do to make more time to pray?

Pray About It

- Ask God to teach you more about His good gift of prayer.

- Tell God why you do or don't enjoy prayer— and ask Him to help you grow.

- Thank God for listening to what you have to say to Him.

. . . .

Lord, my heart overflows with gratitude today. You are the giver of all good things, including prayer. Thank You.

2.
The Ultimate Direct Line

*Now all of us can go to the Father through
Christ by way of the one Holy Spirit.*
EPHESIANS 2:18

Imagine having the phone number of some famous person you admire. Would you have the courage to call or text? Or better yet, imagine if one of your favorite famous people called or texted *you*.

Think having a conversation with a successful actor, singer, or influencer is amazing? Picture this: you're invited to have a personal conversation with the God who created galaxies, stars, and oceans, who breathed life into us and knows the very number of hairs on our heads. Anytime you choose, you can have a heart-to-heart with the Creator of all that is, was, and ever will be. And you can talk about anything you want!

Sometimes prayer can feel like a big, mysterious, holy practice that only the superspiritual adults know how to do. But let me assure you, it's not about fancy words or ancient rituals. You have the same ability to pray as anybody else.

Prayer is simply about showing up just as you are and having a personal conversation with your heavenly Father. So let's go with complete trust to the throne of God.

Think About It

- Why is it helpful to have direct access to God at any time?

- What might prevent you from talking to God in prayer?

- Does the idea of talking to God intimidate you? Why or why not?

Pray About It

- Ask God to remind you to talk to Him.

- Tell God something (anything!) about your day today.

- Thank God for the invitation to connect with Him in prayer.

....

Lord, You tell me I can come to You anytime day or night. Thank You for loving me that much.

3.
A Right and a Responsibility

*Let us go with complete trust to the throne of God.
We will receive His loving-kindness and have His
loving-favor to help us whenever we need it.*
HEBREWS 4:16

You have the freedom to talk to God anytime, anywhere, and about anything. You don't need an appointment, you don't need to wait in line, and you definitely don't need to earn it. It's a birthright, a gift given to you by your loving heavenly Father. You can bring your hopes, fears, joys, and sorrows to Him, knowing that He hears you.

Prayer is a *right* we should never take for granted.

But prayer is also a *responsibility*.

We shouldn't treat prayer as just a magical wish list or a quick fix for our problems. We have a responsibility to approach prayer with humility and gratitude, recognizing that Jesus gave His life so that we could have communion and communication with God.

Once we understand that prayer is a right and a responsibility, we are free to "go with complete trust to the throne of God," just as Hebrews 4:16 tells us. And we can have the confidence that "we will receive His loving-kindness and have His loving-favor to help us whenever we need it."

What an incredible gift from an incredible God!

Think About It

- Do you treat prayer like a gift?
- What do you think it means to approach prayer with humility?
- If God is free to do whatever He wants, why do you think He wants you to talk to Him?

Pray About It

- Make a list of one hope, one fear, one joy, and one sorrow—and talk to God about them.
- Ask God to help you learn to love prayer.
- Express gratitude for God's willingness to help you (because He will!).

....

God, thank You for the promise that when I humbly talk to You in prayer, You will show me kindness and give me help when I need it.

4.
Declaration of Dependence

Those who know Your name will put their trust in You.
For You, O Lord, have never left alone those who look for You.
PSALM 9:10

In school you've probably studied the Declaration of Independence—the historic document that announced America was breaking away from British rule on July 4, 1776. But did you know that when you pray, your prayer is a declaration of *dependence*?

God wants us to depend on Him, and prayer is one way we show Him that we're trusting Him to meet our needs more than we're trusting ourselves. In prayer, we admit our need for God. We humble ourselves before Him, recognizing that we are not self-sufficient—and that's okay. In fact, it's more than okay; it's beautiful. In prayer, dependence is not a weakness; it's a strength.

Depending on God in prayer is an act of faith that says, "Lord, I need You. I can't do this on my own." Thankfully, you don't need to do anything on your own, because God wants to be with you and help you every step of the way. Psalm 9:10 tells us that we can have confidence when we put our trust in God; He won't leave us alone. So there is zero risk in going to God in prayer and trusting Him with our lives.

Isn't that good news?

Think About It

- What is something you need to depend on God for today?

- Why do you think some people believe they can live without prayer?

- When was the last time you felt a strong sense of dependence on God?

Pray About It

- Tell God about something you are thankful for today.

- Ask God to help you with something specific.

- List three reasons why you know you can trust Him.

God, please help my prayers to be a
reflection of my dependence on You.
Thank You for being worthy of my trust.

5.
Partnership with God

*It is good when you pray like this. It pleases
God Who is the One Who saves.*
1 Timothy 2:3

Prayer can feel one-sided, where we rattle off our list of requests and then call it a day.

But prayer is so much more than a monologue.

Prayer is a gracious invitation to partner with God in the important work He is doing in our lives and in the lives of people all over the world. God, being all-powerful, doesn't need us. He can do whatever He wants, but He *chooses* to work with us through prayer. In this special partnership of prayer, we have the privilege of witnessing God's work in the world. When we pray, we play a role in the fulfillment of His plans.

In 1 Timothy 2, the apostle Paul laid out the practical steps the church needed to take in order to prevent false teaching from taking over. He began by discussing prayers for leadership, and then he said, "It is good when you pray like this. It pleases God Who is the One Who saves." Those two sentences illustrate the partnership: it is good to pray, because it pleases God who accomplishes the work.

Prayer is no small privilege. It is partnership with God Almighty.

Think About It

- Why does it sometimes feel like prayer is a one-sided conversation?
- Why do you think God wants to partner with you in prayer?
- How does knowing that God *wants* you to come to Him change your attitude toward prayer?

Pray About It

- Pray about a need in your life.
- Pray about a need in somebody else's life.
- Thank God for the privilege of being His partner in prayer.

Lord, thank You that—though You are self-sufficient and all-powerful—You choose to involve me in Your divine plan.

6.
Change Agent

*Tell your sins to each other. And pray for each other
so you may be healed. The prayer from the heart
of a man right with God has much power.*
JAMES 5:16

Have you ever heard the phrase "change agent"? A change agent is someone who works to bring about big change or improvement in an organization or community. Change agents have the wisdom, skills, and influence to change the way people think or behave.

Though prayer is not a person, it is intended by God to be an agent of change in our lives. Prayer is the means by which God, in His unlimited wisdom and grace, changes us from the inside out.

How does this change work? Isaiah 55 tells us that God's thoughts are not our thoughts and His ways are not our ways. When we pray as God desires, He helps us think and act in ways that honor Him. For example, we admit our weakness, we confess our sin, and we surrender our desires. In these tender moments with God, He works in us to make our thoughts and ways more like His thoughts and ways.

In prayer, we discover the strength to overcome weakness, the wisdom to make good choices, the grace to forgive, and the understanding that we are forgiven.

If you're ever angry, anxious, or sad, stop and pray. See what happens. You'd be surprised how talking to God changes everything.

Think About It

- Do you find some prayers difficult to pray? Why?

- Have you ever changed your mind about something after praying about it?

- Why are God's ways and our ways so different?

Pray About It

- Ask God to help you change something specific in your life.

- Tell God why you trust Him.

- Thank God for His help.

....

Lord, please use prayer to deepen my faith,
increase my trust, and draw me closer to You.

7.
Just the Essentials

But now, O Lord, You are our Father. We are the clay, and You are our pot maker. All of us are the work of Your hand.
ISAIAH 64:8

When you hear the word *worship*, what comes to your mind? Do you think about music, traditions, or services? Although those can be beautiful expressions of our devotion to Him, true worship ultimately involves offering ourselves to God, who made us and sustains us every day.

And at the core of this worship is prayer—the conversation between us and God. Prayer is the means by which we draw near to the throne of grace. It's the way we communicate to our heavenly Father.

It's possible to pray without worshipping—to just go through the motions of prayer. But it's not possible to worship without praying. In prayer, we shift our gaze from ourselves to the maker of the universe, the God who gives us every good thing. We magnify His name and declare His goodness.

So since prayer is essential to worship, we should be careful never to see prayer as a mere warm-up act before the main event. Prayer isn't meant to be a filler or the way to quiet a crowd. We shouldn't rush through it or recite empty words.

Instead, prayer should be essential—a precious conversation between us and God.

Think About It

- How easily does your mind wander during times of prayer at church? Why?

- Do you believe it's impossible to worship without praying? Why or why not?

- Do you ever catch yourself reciting empty words in a prayer before a meal?

Pray About It

- Pray for God to give you a deep desire to pray.

- Ask for help concentrating when you're talking to God.

- Tell God you are willing to learn how to pray in ways that bring Him even more glory.

Lord, please teach me to make prayer a priority in worship. Help me carry on a continuous conversation with You.

8.
Search Terms

*"You will look for Me and find Me, when
you look for Me with all your heart."*
JEREMIAH 29:13

Have you ever listened to a young child pray? Usually, the prayers of a child are heartwarming in their simplicity. But if the children in your life are anything like the children in mine, their prayers are also basically a list of requests: *Help me obey. Help me sleep well. Help my parents know what I want for Christmas.*

And while our prayers may not be quite so obvious, sometimes we can accidentally fall into the trap of viewing our prayers as transactions with God, where we present our requests and hope for swift answers. *Please help me pass tomorrow's test. Please give me friends. Please help me not get into trouble.*

But prayer is more than *requesting*; it is *seeking*.

In prayer, we shouldn't just request solutions to our problems—we should seek the problem solver. We shouldn't just request provision—we should seek the provider. Instead of requesting gifts, we should seek the giver more than the gifts.

It's good to pour out our requests before God, but it's even better to want God Himself.

When we seek God in prayer, we find all we could ever need or desire.

Think About It

- How many of your recent prayers are requests?

- Which do you want more—answers to your requests or God Himself?

- How often do you recite the same prayer from memory?

Pray About It

- Talk to God for two minutes without asking Him for anything.

- Thank God for something He has done for you recently.

- Praise God for one of His attributes you love most (examples: His faithfulness, love, goodness, holiness).

....

God, more than any of the good gifts You give me every day, I want to know and love You best.

9.
The Complete Guide to Prayer

"Pray like this: 'Our Father in heaven, Your name is holy.'"
MATTHEW 6:9

By now you probably know this, but the Bible isn't just a book of stories—it's a masterful guide on how to live the Christian life. And specifically, it teaches us how to pray.

While books, mentors, and small groups are great gifts from God, it's important to understand that if the only prayer instructor you had was your Bible, it would be enough.

When we open the Bible, we find a rich collection of prayers woven throughout its pages, prayers spoken by both ordinary people and giants of the faith. These prayers are helpful because they show us the ways we can talk to God.

We see Abraham pleading on behalf of Sodom and Gomorrah (Genesis 18).

We witness David's raw, honest prayers to God throughout Psalms.

We hear Hannah's heartfelt weeping to God for a son (1 Samuel 1).

And this is only the beginning. The Bible is filled—cover to cover—with dozens of real-life prayers prayed by real-life people. When we read them, we see the sincerity, urgency, and gratitude of the people praying. They show us that prayer isn't about using fancy language or following a strict formula; it's about humbling our hearts and trusting the one we are praying to.

Think About It

- What is your favorite prayer recorded in the Bible?

- Why do you think we have so many different examples of prayer in the Bible?

- Why is it tempting to think we need to use fancy language when we pray?

Pray About It

- Thank God for the gift of the Bible as a prayer mentor.

- Tell God you want to be sincere and honest in the way you talk to Him.

- Ask God to help you with anything you find difficult about praying.

Thank You, heavenly Father, for the priceless gift of Your Word and the way it teaches me how to pray.

10.
What Did Jesus Do?

"When you pray, go into a room by yourself. After you have shut the door, pray to your Father Who is in secret. Then your Father Who sees in secret will reward you."
MATTHEW 6:6

Jesus set the greatest example in scripture of fervent and heartfelt prayer.

In addition to teaching the Lord's Prayer, which we will look at later in this book, He set the example with His life of how to commune with His Father. Throughout the Gospels, we see Him withdrawing to solitary places to pray. He would spend entire nights in conversation with His Father, seeking guidance, requesting strength, and pledging obedience. What a powerful reminder that even Jesus felt the need to connect with God in prayer.

One important takeaway from Jesus' prayers is the fact that He didn't hide His emotions or sugarcoat His words. In His famous prayer in the garden of Gethsemane, for example, He poured out His heart in agony, yet He surrendered to the will of His Father.

His famous words—"Not My will but Yours be done"—are a lesson to us in vulnerability and trust. We would be wise to pray the same way.

Think About It

- Why do you think prayer was important to Jesus?
- Why do you believe Jesus needed to withdraw to quiet places to pray?
- What is most important in your regular conversations with God?

Pray About It

- Ask God to teach you how to pray like Jesus.
- Remember that the same God to whom Jesus prayed in the garden of Gethsemane wants to hear from you.
- Spend time telling God what's on your heart today.

....

God, please teach me to pray like Jesus prayed—not my will but Yours be done.

11.
At a Loss for Words

*In the same way, the Holy Spirit helps us where we
are weak. We do not know how to pray or what we
should pray for, but the Holy Spirit prays to God for
us with sounds that cannot be put into words.*

ROMANS 8:26

Have you ever bowed your head to pray and been unsure
what to say? Maybe you're carrying a hurt that's too big to
say out loud. Or maybe you don't even know what outcome
you want in a situation because any outcome will be difficult.

Here's the good news: when you don't have the words,
when your heart is too heavy, or when your mind is too confused to form sentences, the Holy Spirit prays on your behalf.

It sounds too good to be true, but Romans 8:26 assures
us that the Spirit communicates with God on our behalf in a
language that goes beyond words. The Spirit speaks to God in
a language of deep groans, unspoken longing, and emotions
too complex for human language.

In other words, God loves you so much that even when
you don't have the ability to tell Him what you need, He will
communicate with the Spirit so that your prayers are still

heard and understood. Whether or not you realize it, God is always working on your behalf.

Think About It

- Why is it hard to pray when your heart is broken?
- Why do you believe the Spirit wants to pray on your behalf?
- Why is it important to keep talking to God during difficult times?

Pray About It

- Ask God to help you pray even on hard days.
- Thank God for sending the Spirit to help.
- Spend time telling God what's on your heart today.

....

God, thank You for the help of the Spirit when I am wordless, and thank You for the assurance that my prayers— even in my silence—are heard and cherished by You.

12.
All Good Things

"You are bad and you know how to give good things to your children. How much more will your Father in heaven give good things to those who ask Him?"
MATTHEW 7:11

If you really, *really* want something from your parents, how do you ask for it? Maybe you'd first do something you knew they liked (such as cleaning your room or finishing your homework). You might use a sweet tone of voice and tell them about your good grades or your recent track record of great decisions. You might assume that how you ask will determine how they answer.

We can be tempted to talk to God in prayer in similar ways. Sometimes we incorrectly believe that how we pray—the tone we use, the words we choose, the holiness we exhibit—will determine whether we get the answer from God that we want. That's often how it works with humans.

But prayer isn't about manipulation—we can't control God to get what we want. Prayer is about alignment, agreeing with God about what we need.

Like Matthew 7:11 tells us that if sinful human beings know how to give good gifts to their kids, how much better is a perfect God at giving good gifts to His children when they ask?

When you pray, is your greatest goal to get what you want? Or to get what God wants for you? He will give you only what is best.

Think About It

- Does "God's best" always mean we get what we want?
- Why is it wiser to let God decide what He gives?
- How can a painful answer from God still be a good answer?

Pray About It

- Ask God to help you trust His decisions for your life.
- Thank God for being a good Father.
- Offer God your willingness to believe He wants what is best.

....

Forgive me for thinking You have to say yes to my prayers, Father. Instead, help me say yes to following Your plan.

13.
Wait and See

*Our life is lived by faith. We do not live
by what we see in front of us.*
2 Corinthians 5:7

When it comes to conversation with God, we have two responsibilities: pray and trust.

Prayer, as we've seen already in this book, is our opportunity to pour out our hearts and to lay our hopes and fears at the feet of the God who knows us best. Prayer is a wonderful privilege.

But here's the catch: prayer doesn't always get the immediate answers or visible solutions that we request. And that's where the second responsibility—trust—becomes important. Trust requires us to surrender control, to release our need for an immediate response, and to accept the mystery of God's timing and plan.

Prayer and trust go hand in hand. When we pray, we're saying, "God, I'm giving this situation to You. I'm laying everything out here, trusting that You know what's best for me." It's an acknowledgment that we don't have all the answers, but we serve the God who does.

As children of God, we live by faith and not by sight. God invites us to pray and trust—to accept these two responsibilities with open hands and willing hearts, knowing that we are held and loved beyond measure.

Think About It

- Which do you find harder to do—pray or trust?

- Why is prayer more than just asking for what we want?

- How can you become more intentional about trusting God with your requests?

Pray About It

- Ask God to give you more courage when you talk to Him.

- Invite God to show you where you need to have more trust in His plan.

- Determine that you will pray today and then wait for God's response.

God, I trust Your wisdom and love, knowing that You see the bigger picture, even when my vision is clouded.

14.
Praise to the Skies

*Let us give thanks all the time to God through
Jesus Christ. Our gift to Him is to give thanks.
Our lips should always give thanks to His name.*
HEBREWS 13:15

When you hear the word *praise*, what comes to mind? Maybe you think about joyful music, grateful testimonies, or Sunday services. And you wouldn't be wrong. But did you know *prayer* can and should also be offered to God as praise?

Prayer isn't simply a laundry list of requests we bring to God. Prayer also serves as an intentional opportunity to acknowledge His goodness and holiness. In prayer, we lift our hearts in gratitude, awe, and reverence to our Creator.

In Hebrews 13:15, we're invited to "give thanks all the time to God through Jesus." So every time we speak to God—whether in moments of joy or sorrow, seeking or surrender—we should offer up words of praise for who He is and what He has done in our lives.

When we look back and remember what God has already done for us—when He answered previous prayers, brought us through hard seasons, poured His grace on us in moments of need—it strengthens our trust. It reminds us that the same God who was faithful in the past will be faithful today.

Think About It

- Does praise ever seem like the hardest part of prayer?

- What is something praiseworthy that God has done for you in the past?

- What is something about God's character you can praise Him for right now?

Pray About It

- Think of three things you are thankful for and use each one as a reason for praise.

- Ask God to help you remember His goodness.

- Take note of life events and use these memories to inspire praise toward God.

. . . .

God, please help me remember that prayer isn't just for asking—it's also for praising. You are so, so good.

15.
Not to Worry

Do not worry. Learn to pray about everything.
Give thanks to God as you ask Him for what you need.
PHILIPPIANS 4:6

Have you ever carried something really heavy? Picture it—that overfull backpack, that suitcase bursting at the seams. You know the feeling, right? Remember how good it felt to finally set that weight down? With the burden lifted and your shoulders unburdened, you can breathe freely again.

Did you know one of the heaviest burdens we carry on a regular basis is worry? Just like we fill that backpack or suitcase with stuff, we fill our hearts and minds with concerns, anxieties, and issues we can't control. Sometimes we don't even realize we're doing it. And just like a heavy bag, it can wear us down, making life so much harder than God intended it to be.

Thankfully, God has given us a way to set our worries down: prayer.

In prayer, we have the opportunity to surrender our worries and hand them over to a loving, all-knowing, and all-powerful God who is strong enough to carry them for us without ever getting tired. And just like taking off the heavy backpack, surrendering our worries can result in immediate relief. Philippians 4:6 tells us, "Do not worry. Learn to pray about everything."

Worried about something today? Give it to God in prayer.

Think About It

- When you're worried about something, do you naturally stop to pray about it?
- Why do you think Philippians 4:6 links thanking God in prayer with not worrying?
- Is it easier for you to talk to God or to your friends about your worries?

Pray About It

- Tell God about any worries you are carrying today.
- Ask God to remind you to pray when you're tempted to worry.
- Thank God for something He's done for you today.

....

God, please teach me to surrender my worries to You, knowing that You are the source of true peace and comfort.

16.
Peace of Mind

The peace of God is much greater than the human mind can understand. This peace will keep your hearts and minds through Christ Jesus.

PHILIPPIANS 4:7

In the last entry, we read about Philippians 4:6, "Do not worry. Learn to pray about everything."

But the next verse—Philippians 4:7—shows us the result of making the decision to pray about everything: "The peace of God is much greater than the human mind can understand. This peace will keep your hearts and minds through Christ Jesus." Many people call this "the peace that passes understanding." Maybe you've heard that phrase. But what exactly is this type of peace?

The peace in Philippians 4:7 can be received only from God. It isn't rooted in the world's logic or human reasoning. It doesn't depend on having all the answers. Instead, it relies on trusting the goodness of God.

Peace that passes understanding steadies our hearts in the face of chaos. It calms us down when we're troubled. It reminds us that we are secure in Christ—no matter how insecure we feel about anything else. The reason this peace passes human understanding is because it has nothing to do with our circumstances and everything to do with our security in Christ.

Do you want this peace? Pray about everything.

Think About It

- Can you think of a time you had peace that didn't make sense?

- Who is someone in the Bible who had peace that passed human understanding?

- Why do you think it's tempting to look for peace in all the wrong places?

Pray About It

- Thank God for caring about your worries.

- Tell God about any difficult circumstances you're facing.

- Ask God to give you His perfect peace.

Lord, in the midst of life's challenges and uncertainties, please give me the peace that can come only from You.

17.
A Thousand Thanks

*Praise the Lord, O my soul. And all that is within
me, praise His holy name. Praise the Lord, O my
soul. And forget none of His acts of kindness.*

PSALM 103:1–2

When we truly stop to consider all God has done for us, we should be filled with an overwhelming sense of awe and wonder. Here we are, with all our imperfections, our messiness, our quirks and flaws—and yet we are cherished, adored, and loved by a gracious God who is absolutely perfect. He is totally indescribable in His goodness.

Prayer is our way to connect with the God of the universe and to acknowledge with gratitude that everything we have, everything we are, and everything we hope to be is *from* Him and *for* Him.

God doesn't need our thanks—He doesn't need anything. But expressing our gratitude to Him changes us. It changes our hearts and reminds us who is responsible for everything good that we have been given.

If we're truly thinking about God and His goodness the way we should, then prayers of gratitude will flow from our hearts and mouths automatically. Our prayers should be a continual song of thanksgiving to God.

Think About It

- Is it easy or hard for you to offer thanksgiving to God? Why?
- Why is it easy for us to forget to thank God for what He provides?
- When was the last time you thanked God for His goodness to you?

Pray About It

- Thank God for three ways He's provided for you in the past.
- Thank God for three ways He's providing for you right now.
- Thank God for three ways He'll provide for you in the future.

. . . .

God, please let my life be a living testimony to Your goodness and a reflection of the gratitude that fills my heart.

18.
Fellowship of the Forgiven

If we tell Him our sins, He is faithful and we
can depend on Him to forgive us of our sins.
He will make our lives clean from all sin.

1 JOHN 1:9

One reason prayer is a gift in our lives is that we have a way to repent of sin and be made right with God. Prayer is our way to seek forgiveness and reconciliation with our heavenly Father.

When you know you've sinned—when you've fallen short of God's perfect standards—what do you do? Do you ignore it? Deny it? Acknowledge it?

None of us are exempt from sinning or falling short of the mark—which is why Jesus had to die for every single one of us. Thankfully, God's grace is abundant, His mercy is unfathomable, and His love is unending. So when we sin, the best thing we can do next is go to God in prayer.

How do you pray for forgiveness? Pour out your heart honestly and vulnerably. Confess your wrongdoing and seek God's forgiveness.

And you know what? God, in all His grace and mercy, doesn't turn us away. He doesn't shame or condemn us. No, He welcomes us with open arms, ready to offer the gift of forgiveness. First John 1:9 promises that if we go to God for forgiveness, He will make our lives clean from all sin. Isn't that amazing?

Think About It

- Do you have anything you need to ask God to forgive you for today?
- How is the promise in 1 John 1:9 a wonderful gift?
- How can you praise God for His forgiveness?

Pray About It

- Thank God for His forgiveness.
- Ask God to forgive you for the ways you've fallen short of His perfect standard.
- Thank God for His great love.

. . . .

Lord, thank You for the fresh beginnings
that Your forgiveness provides.

19.
The Greatest Gift

*First of all, I ask you to pray much for all
men and to give thanks for them.*
1 TIMOTHY 2:1

Picture this: You talk to a friend who's going through something really difficult. What do you do?

You may not have the money, the answers, or the influence needed to fix the situation, but you can still make a profound difference. What's the greatest thing you can do for people in need? You can pray to God.

Reaching out to God on someone else's behalf is a great kindness. Psalm 50:10 tells us that God owns the cattle on a thousand hills, meaning everything in this world belongs to Him. God *does* have the resources needed to fix whatever situation your friend is facing. So by talking to God, you're talking to someone who can actually make things better.

The key isn't just *telling* people you'll pray for them but actually *doing* it. When you're confronted with someone else's suffering, you have a powerful tool at your disposal. Praying for others is an act of compassion, and it can change lives.

Let's pray for people with faith in the God who listens, cares, and moves mountains.

Think About It

- Why do you think people don't consider praying for others to be helpful?

- What does it mean to know that someone is praying for you?

- How is praying for other people an act of humility?

Pray About It

- Pray for someone in your life who needs God's help today.

- Ask God to show you ways you can faithfully pray for others.

- Thank God for people who have prayed for you in the past.

God, thank You for the gift of prayer and the ability to intercede for others. Please remind me to pray for those in need.

20.
Time for Revival!

*Will You not bring us back to life again so that
Your people may be happy in You? Show us Your
loving-kindness, O Lord, and save us.*

PSALM 85:6–7

In the quiet spaces of our lives, where the noise of the world
fades away, we find a place to commune with God in prayer.
And in these moments of sweet surrender, we learn an important truth: prayer can lead to personal revival.

Revival is a word often associated with American religious
history. Christians sometimes talk about revival as a distant
historical event. But revival shouldn't be distant to us at all.

Revival is simply a renewed or revitalized interest in and
commitment to our faith. Sometimes it results in significant,
positive change for an entire community of people, but it
should also be simple, daily growth in the life of a child of God.

The beauty of personal revival is that it is not reserved for
a select few but available to all who seek it. Through prayer,
our souls are refreshed, our faith is rekindled, and our hearts
are recommitted to love and serve God.

Prayer is a catalyst to spiritual growth.

Think About It

- When you hear the word *revival*, what comes to mind?

- Have you ever asked God to do a work of revival in your heart?

- Why is revival something we should want in our lives?

Pray About It

- Thank God for His work of revival in Christian history.

- Ask God to do revival work in your heart today.

- Ask God to do His revival work in your country, city, church, and home.

....

Lord, I long for a revival in my heart, one that overflows into every aspect of my life. Please help my thoughts, words, and actions to please You.

21.
You Are Invited

Come close to God and He will come close to you. Wash your hands, you sinners. Clean up your hearts, you who want to follow the sinful ways of the world and God at the same time.
JAMES 4:8

You are invited to spend time with someone who knows you inside and out, who loves you with a never-ending, indescribable, unshakable love, and who wants to spend time with you. This invitation isn't just any invitation; this invitation is from God Himself.

Prayer is your invitation to draw close to God, who knows you best.

In prayer, you can shed the layers of self-protection, strip away the masks you wear for the world, and stand before your creator God as you truly are. He already knows everything there is to know about you, so what would be the point of pretending to be anything else? In prayer, you can't impress or pretend; you simply come as you are, just as you were created.

Prayer isn't about perfect words or eloquent phrases either. It's about a heart-to-heart connection with your Father—about spending time with God, who offers perfect direction, comfort, and hope.

James 4:8 promises that if we come close to God, He will come close to us. The invitation is yours for the taking.

Think About It

- When you talk to God, are you comfortable being honest with Him?

- Why is it a human temptation to look better or different than we actually are?

- How is it comforting to know God will come close to you when you come close to Him?

Pray About It

- Share one true thought with God.

- Share one true feeling with God.

- Share one true struggle with God.

. . . .

Thank You, God, for drawing near, for loving me, and for inviting me to spend time with You. I love You.

22.
Now You're Talking

*The Lord spoke to Moses face to face,
as a man speaks to his friend.*
EXODUS 33:11

By now you know that prayer is many things. It's a lifeline, a place of refuge, a source of comfort, and a pathway to deeper connection with God. It's the way God works in and through us, and it's the heartbeat of our relationship with Him.

But at the end of the day, prayer is simply conversation with God.

How do you talk to your friends or family members that you love? Well, God wants you to have that same desire and level of comfort when you talk to Him. Like Moses in Exodus 33, you are invited to talk to God as a man speaks to his friend.

Sometimes we can place so much pressure on ourselves when it comes to prayer that suddenly it becomes intimidating. We might feel like we need to have the perfect words, the most eloquent phrases, or a peaceful state of mind to approach God. But prayer is simply conversation. God wants you to talk to Him about anything and everything! No situation is too big, nor is any detail too small.

If you're ever too overwhelmed or intimidated to pray, remind yourself: prayer is simply a conversation.

Think About It

- Why might prayer become intimidating? Why is that silly?

- Have you ever caught yourself saying eloquent or flowery things in prayer just because you think you should?

- Why do you think some people change the tone of their voice when praying?

Pray About It

- Tell God about your day.

- Ask God to remind you throughout the day to talk to Him.

- Thank God for the incredible privilege of being able to talk to Him as His child.

....

Help me to never take this privilege of prayer for granted, Lord, but to approach it with a humble and thankful heart.

23.
Eight Important Words

He said, "Father, if it can be done, take away what must happen to Me. Even so, not what I want, but what You want."

LUKE 22:42

One reason prayer is a great gift to us is that it helps us align our desires with God's will.

How does that work?

We pray sincerely. We tell God all the dreams we're hoping for, all the temptations we're struggling with, and all the ways we'd love to see Him work in our lives. But we don't stop there. We end each of those prayers the way Jesus ended His prayer to God before He was crucified, saying, "Not what I want, but what You want." If we mean them, those eight words can be really hard to say. I don't know about you, but I don't like surrendering my will to anyone else, even when I know it's the right choice to make.

But guess what? God's will is far better than ours, *every time*. Sometimes what we thought we needed or wanted turns out to be nothing like what we hoped. God's "no" can actually be a relief down the road when we better understand what we were asking.

God knows what's best, so we can trust Him.

Think About It

- Why is surrendering to God's will so difficult?

- Do you believe God is being kind or unkind when He says "no" to a request?

- Does it make it easier for you to trust God if you know He loves you?

Pray About It

- Ask God for courage to want His will more than your own.

- Tell God about something you've learned about prayer while reading this book.

- Practice ending your prayer time by telling God, "Not what I want, but what You want."

....

Father, please give me the strength and grace to do Your will, even when it leads me in unexpected directions.

24.
In Safe Hands

*I will say to the Lord, "You are my safe and
strong place, my God, in Whom I trust."*
PSALM 91:2

Who do you talk to *first* on really hard days? Do you talk
to your friends, your parents, or your counselor? Those are
good choices. We should absolutely talk to someone we trust
when we're struggling. But did you know God wants you to
talk to *Him*?

In moments of chaos and anxiety, prayer is your lifeline to
God. Psalm 91:2 tells us that God is our safe and strong place.
When you're overwhelmed, uncertain, or just plain scared
about the future, God wants you to pray. He knows better
than anybody what you're experiencing and what you need.

But what *specifically* should you pray for when you're
struggling? Here are a few ideas:

Pour out your heart to God in an honest and transparent
way. Admit your need for His help, acknowledging that you
can do nothing apart from Him. Pray for strength and the
ability to endure with patience and perseverance, knowing that
God is refining your character through the challenges you face.

Trust that God knows, hears, and cares about anything that overwhelms you. When you talk to God in prayer, you're in safe hands.

Think About It

- What do you typically do when you're overwhelmed? Do you bottle up your feelings or talk about them with someone?

- Why does it honor God when we take our troubles to Him?

- How does it dishonor God when we don't talk to Him about our struggles?

Pray About It

- Thank God for wanting to help you.

- Ask God to help you see the value in going to Him first.

- Talk to God about anything troubling you today.

Thank You for being my safe place, my refuge, and my rock in times of trouble.

25.
As Long as You Live

*I will praise the Lord as long as I live. I will
sing praises to my God as long as I live.*
PSALM 146:2

More than just a religious ritual or a transaction with God, prayer is a way to convey our deepest love and appreciation for our heavenly Father.

Stop and consider this truth for a minute: you get to speak directly to the God who formed you, protects you, and sacrificed His only Son so that you can live forever with Him.

Isn't that amazing?

Throughout history, many people have made sacrifices for us, yet we are unable to thank them. With God, we get to express our love and our appreciation that He is the source of all that is right in our lives. Like the writer of Psalm 146:2, we get to praise the Lord as long as we live. And when we truly begin to understand all He has done and is doing for us, it will be our great privilege and joy to express our love for Him in prayer.

Not sure where to begin? Start here: "Lord, thank You for the gift of salvation through Your Son, Jesus Christ. I don't understand why You did it for me, but I'm very thankful, and I love You."

Think About It

- Why is it easy to take for granted all God does for us?

- When was the last time you told God you love Him?

- What can you do to make praise a part of every prayer?

Pray About It

- Thank God for something specific He has done for you.

- Praise God for what He means to you.

- Tell God you love Him.

*I love You, Lord, not just for what You do
for me but for who You are—the Almighty,
the Creator, my Savior, and my friend.*

26.
Forever and a Day

*"May Your holy nation come. What You want done,
may it be done on earth as it is in heaven."*
MATTHEW 6:10

You already understand that prayer is a great gift to us for many reasons. Here's one more: prayer helps us develop an eternal perspective. Though it may feel otherwise when you're young, this lifetime isn't forever.

The day is coming when—if we've trusted Jesus for our salvation—we will leave all our earthly concerns behind and spend eternity with God. This truth isn't meant to create fear or dread, but it should encourage us to love God better and to cultivate a closer relationship with Him. We'll want to invest our greatest time and energy into things that truly matter from an eternal perspective.

In Matthew 6, when Jesus taught about prayer on the side of a mountain, He linked the earthly to the heavenly, because prayer is the way this world touches the next. When we pray, we shift our focus from only what matters here on earth to all that matters most in heaven—from the worldly to the divine.

In Christ, we have everything we need for now and for all eternity.

Think About It

- When you think about eternity, what comes to mind?

- Are you filled with joy or dread when you think about spending eternity with God?

- Have you trusted in Jesus for your salvation, and do you know that your eternity with Him is certain?

Pray About It

- Spend time talking to God about what matters most to you.

- Ask God to give you an eternal perspective.

- Talk to God about something that is eternal and not just earthly.

Help me, Lord, to set my heart on things above, to fix my gaze on the eternal truths of Your Word, and to seek You above all else.

27.
Keep in Touch

The Lord is near to all who call on Him,
to all who call on Him in truth.
PSALM 145:18

Since prayer is the primary way we communicate with our Creator, what happens to our relationship with Him when we fail to pray?

What happens when you avoid talking to your friends? How would you feel if someone called you her best friend and then didn't ever talk to you or sit with you at lunch or hang out with you after school?

Like avoiding conversations with our friends or family, avoiding prayer makes our connection with God grow distant, and we may feel less connected to Him. Just as sharing our joys and sorrows with friends and family deepens our connections, pouring out our hearts to God in prayer deepens our relationship with Him.

Without prayer, we risk becoming spiritually isolated and alone, detaching ourselves from the source of our truest strength and help. Often, when we feel like God is distant, it isn't because He's moved away from us—it's because we haven't talked to Him in prayer.

Do you want a close relationship with God? Psalm 145:18 promises that God will draw near to all who talk to Him in prayer. It's that simple.

Think About It

- Do you find it easy or hard to pray consistently?
- Can you tell a difference in your relationship with God when you pray regularly?
- Why do you think Satan doesn't want you to pray?

Pray About It

- Tell God any reasons you struggle to pray.
- Ask God to help you talk to Him more often.
- Thank God for the gift of His friendship.

....

God, thank You for being a patient and loving listener, always ready to hear my words and the concerns on my heart. Thank You for being my friend.

28.
The Door Is Always Open

You must pray at all times as the Holy Spirit leads you to pray. Pray for the things that are needed. You must watch and keep on praying. Remember to pray for all Christians.
EPHESIANS 6:18

One of the most extraordinary things about prayer is that it's not limited to any particular time or place. What's more, you don't need a secret code to access heaven. No, prayer is an open invitation, an ever-present connection between you and God.

You can pray in the quiet of your early morning before breakfast or school or work. You can pray in the middle of a noisy room while chaos happens all around you. You can talk to God at night when your mind is too full or concerned to sleep. . . . Talk to God at any time and at any place!

Just as the apostle Paul wrote to the Christians of Ephesus in the scripture above, we should pray at all times as the Holy Spirit leads us to pray. The invitation is always available, and the conversation is never-ending.

And just think of it: after spending a lifetime talking to God here on earth, you will go to live with Him in heaven, where the conversation will continue for eternity.

Think About It

- Where could you talk to God today that you haven't talked to Him before?

- Is there a specific time of your day when you feel most connected to God in prayer?

- What do you understand about God because of His invitation to pray anytime and anywhere?

Pray About It

- Pray at least once in the morning.

- Pray at least once in the afternoon.

- Pray at least once in the evening.

Father, help me to be mindful of this beautiful privilege, to remember that I can pray to You anywhere and at any time.

29.
Safe and Sound

Our fight is not with people. It is against the leaders and the powers and the spirits of darkness in this world. It is against the demon world that works in the heavens.
EPHESIANS 6:12

As children of God, we know that our enemy on this earth is not simply flesh and blood—it's the same enemy Adam and Eve faced in the garden. Satan and those who agree with him seek to undermine our faith and hinder God's purposes.

While we shouldn't spend a lot of time talking or thinking about darkness, it's important to understand that we should take it seriously.

One weapon God has given us to fight those who would seek to destroy our faith is the tool of prayer. Our prayer life should be anchored in scripture, rooted in worship, and marked by closeness with God. To use this tool of prayer as an effective weapon against evil, we must pray actively and fervently. We should pray for others as well as ourselves.

In Jesus' famous Sermon on the Mount, He gave us the example of how to pray in this way. He said, "And lead us not into temptation, but deliver us from the evil one" (Matthew 6:13 NIV). This too should be our prayer.

Thankfully, God is willing and able to protect us.

Think About It

- How does prayer work as a weapon against darkness?

- Do you believe God actively protects you from sin and evil?

- Why do you think Jesus mentioned evil in His example of how to pray?

Pray About It

- Thank God for giving you the tool of prayer.

- Ask God to keep you safe from those who do evil.

- Ask God to protect people you love.

....

*Lord, thank You for guarding me from harm
and for protecting me from countless threats
and challenges I don't even see or understand.
You are absolutely trustworthy, and I love You.*

30.
Always the Next Right Thing

*Trust in the Lord with all your heart, and do not trust
in your own understanding. Agree with Him in all
your ways, and He will make your paths straight.*
PROVERBS 3:5–6

Sometimes life throws us curveballs that leave us confused
or uncertain.

Maybe you're given an opportunity but you don't know if
you should take it. Maybe you're put in an awkward situation
and you don't know how to respond. Maybe you wonder what
you should do in the future about big decisions like college
or employment or marriage.

What is the next right thing to do? Pray about it.

Prayer is one way we receive God's guidance in big and
small matters. When we pray, we're acknowledging that we
are limited in our understanding, while God's wisdom is
boundless. Even if we don't use those exact words, the very act
of praying communicates to God that we know we don't have
all the answers. We take our concerns and questions to God,
ask Him what we should do, and wait to see how He leads.

Important note: God *wants* you to know and do His will, so when you ask, He will show you the next right step at the perfect time.

Think About It

- Have you ever prayed about a big decision and received a clear answer from God?

- Why is praying proof that we know we don't have all the answers we need?

- What are some examples of big decisions God wants us to pray about?

Pray About It

- Ask God for wisdom about something big in your life.

- Ask God for wisdom about something small in your life.

- Thank God for His promise that He will direct your path.

. . . .

Father, thank You for Your guidance. In all of life's decisions, I know I can come to You for direction and wisdom.

31.
No Other Name

"Whatever you ask in My name, I will do it so the shining-greatness of the Father may be seen in the Son."

JOHN 14:13

Why do we pray in Jesus' name? Is it just a formality? Is it tradition?

Jesus is the one who, by His perfect life and death on the cross, purchased for us our access to God. When we pray the words "in Jesus' name," we are really saying, "Because of what Jesus did for me, I am able to bring my requests to You, God." Jesus stands in the gap for us, bridging the space between us and God, offering His own righteousness and grace to make our prayers heard and accepted.

So praying in Jesus' name is a great and costly privilege. It cost Jesus His life.

When we pray in Jesus' name, we're acknowledging that we have access to the Creator of the universe, not because of our own merit, but because of the incredible gift of grace through Christ.

When you pray in Jesus' name, know you aren't just uttering empty words; you are affirming your faith, acknowledging

Jesus' role as your mediator, and embracing the incredible gift of grace made available to you through Christ.

What a gift it is!

Think About It

- Why do you think it honors Jesus when we pray in His name?

- Why is it a great privilege for us to pray in Jesus' name?

- When you hear people use Jesus' name casually, how do you feel? Why?

Pray About It

- Thank God for access to Him through prayer.

- Thank God for the gift of salvation, made possible through His Son.

- Tell God what it means to you to be able to pray in Jesus' name.

....

God, thank You for the privilege to approach You with confidence, knowing that through the name of Your beloved Son my prayers are heard and answered.

32.
Word for Word

"When you pray, do not say the same thing over and over again making long prayers like the people who do not know God. They think they are heard because their prayers are long."
MATTHEW 6:7

The Lord's Prayer, recorded for us in Matthew 6:9–13, was originally given by Jesus to His disciples as a blueprint for how to pray. Today, it serves as a helpful template when we consider the kinds of things we should bring before the Lord.

But the Lord's Prayer is not meant to be a mantra or a mindless repetition. It's intended to be a model. Matthew 6:9 encourages us to "pray *like* this," but it never requires us to "pray these exact words."

The Lord's Prayer offers a clear structure for the most important aspects of prayer: acknowledging God's holiness, requesting His guidance, asking for daily provision, seeking forgiveness, and acknowledging His sovereignty. But He also wants to hear those things from you in your own words. The goal was never for the Lord's Prayer to be recited mechanically. There is nothing magical or mystical about the prayer recorded for us in Matthew 6.

Instead of reciting a memorized prayer, we should pour out our own thoughts, feelings, and requests within the basic framework of this example.

God doesn't want a mantra from you—He wants a relationship with you.

Think About It

- Why do you think God wants you to pray in your own words?
- Is it easier to pray in your own words or to recite a memorized prayer?
- Do you ever notice yourself saying the same things when you pray?

Pray About It

- Thank God for giving us an example prayer.
- Think through everything you tell God.
- Tell God something you haven't told Him before.

Lord, thank You for including such a beautiful example of how to pray in the Bible.

33.
Dust and Breath

When I look up and think about Your heavens, the work of Your fingers, the moon and the stars, which You have set in their place, what is man, that You think of him, the son of man that You care for him?

PSALM 8:3–4

There's something incredibly beautiful about approaching the Creator of the universe with a humble heart. Consider this: when you pray, you're talking to the God who flung the stars into the sky and spoke the world into existence and holds us all in the palm of His hand.

When we remember who God is and who we are, praying with humility is the right and natural response.

We have no right to make demands of God. We are dust and breath, here today and gone tomorrow. It's easy to forget our place in the grand scheme of things, to let our egos swell and think we can boss God around. But we are not in charge—God is in charge.

Praying with humility means recognizing our smallness and God's vastness. It means acknowledging that we don't have all the answers and that God's wisdom far exceeds our own.

It means coming to God with respect and awe, just like we're stepping on holy ground.

Think About It

- Why is it important to remember who God is?
- How does being humble help you pray better?
- Why is it good that God is bigger, stronger, and wiser than we are?

Pray About It

- Praise God for who He is.
- Ask God to forgive you if you've made demands of Him.
- Thank Him for being good and trustworthy.

....

God, I come before You with a humble heart, recognizing my limitations and imperfections. You are the source of all wisdom, love, and grace, and I am grateful You care for me.

34.
When God Says, "Yes!"

We are sure that if we ask anything that He wants us to have, He will hear us.

1 JOHN 5:14

One reason we pray is that there's truly nothing better than bringing a request to God, pouring out our hearts and desires to Him, and receiving the answer we seek. Through prayer, we sometimes—though not always—get to experience the joy of His "Yes!" And it's the greatest feeling in the world.

Have you ever prayed for something—help finding something you lost, for example—and when you discovered it, you knew God was the one who led you to what you needed?

In those moments, when God responds with a "yes", we experience a profound connection to Him that we would have missed if we hadn't asked Him for His help. Sure, He may have chosen to help us out of the goodness and kindness of His heart; but by praying, we get to share that tender moment with Him.

He is a good God who delights to give us good things. First John 5:14 tells us that if we ask anything that God wants us to have, He will hear us.

So ask.

Think About It

- When was the last time you asked God for something and received His "yes"?

- Do you believe God wants to give you good things?

- What stops you from asking for His help more often?

Pray About It

- Ask God for something specific that you need.

- Thank God for the times He's helped you without your knowledge of it.

- Ask God to help you pay attention to the things He says yes to.

....

Father, I am humbled by Your willingness to hear my requests and respond with "Yes!" You know what I need, and Your kindness fills me with awe and gratitude.

35.
Who's the Boss?

Pray for kings and all others who are in power over us so we might live quiet God-like lives in peace.
1 TIMOTHY 2:2

Did you know that God wants you to pray for the authority figures in your life? Scripture tells us that the leaders in our lives—politicians, bosses, teachers, mentors, parents—have important work to do and need our prayers.

The Bible paints a vivid picture of the responsibilities and challenges leaders face in guiding, teaching, and caring for others. They are entrusted with important work that impacts the lives of those they lead. Leading is no small task. The leaders in your life are accountable to God for the decisions they make.

So what should we pray for, specifically? We should ask God to give leaders strength to lead with integrity, wisdom to make good decisions, and compassion to consider the well-being of everyone in their care. First Timothy 2:2 indicates that praying for our leadership can help create peace in our own lives, so it benefits us when we pray for those in authority.

Whether or not we think they always do a good job—and whether or not we would do things differently—we should pray for our leaders. God is the ultimate authority, and He can help them—and us—do what is right.

Think About It

- Why do you think God wants you to pray for the leaders in your life?

- How can God help leaders do what is right?

- How can your prayer influence other people?

Pray About It

- Thank God for good leaders in your life.

- Ask God to give leaders wisdom to make good decisions.

- Pray for some of your leaders by name.

....

Thank You, God, for the leaders in my life. I trust that You have placed each one in my life for a reason. Help me remember to faithfully pray for each one.

36.
Unwinding Anxiety

*He who lives in the safe place of the Most High will be
in the shadow of the All-powerful. I will say to the Lord,
"You are my safe and strong place, my God, in Whom I trust."*
PSALM 91:1–2

What do you do when you feel anxious? When you are confronted with a situation beyond your control and your mind becomes trapped by worry and fear, where do you go? Who do you talk to?

It is good to talk to trustworthy adults in moments of anxiety. We should never try to handle anxiety on our own. But in addition to talking to helpful adults, we should also talk to God. Prayer is a means God has given us to fight anxiety.

In prayer, we give our paralyzing fears to the God who upholds the universe by the power of His word. In prayer, we acknowledge our dependence on God, who holds all things in His hands.

There is nothing in your life He cannot handle.

In this broken world we face challenges, heartaches, and uncertainties that can leave us feeling anxious. But in the midst of it all, we have a God who is steadfast, unchanging, and all-powerful. God is never up in heaven wringing His hands, wondering how on earth He's going to fix a situation. No, He's waiting and ready to handle anything that comes our way.

Next time you're anxious. . .*pray*.

Think About It

- How do you typically respond to moments of anxiety?

- Why does prayer relieve our anxious feelings?

- Can you think of anyone in the Bible who found peace in difficult circumstances by praying?

Pray About It

- Thank God for inviting you to bring your concerns to Him.

- Tell God about anything overwhelming you today.

- Trust God to handle whatever difficult circumstances you are facing.

Lord, I give You my biggest fears, worries, and uncertainties. I trust in Your wisdom and unchanging love. In exchange for my anxiety, please give me Your perfect peace as I trust You.

37.
More Than a Suggestion

Be happy in your hope. Do not give up when trouble comes. Do not let anything stop you from praying.
ROMANS 12:12

Prayer, though it is a gift in our lives, is not simply for our benefit. Prayer is also an act of obedience to God. The Bible doesn't merely suggest that we pray—it commands us to pray.

When we come to God in prayer, we are submitting ourselves to His divine authority in our lives. And this act of submission glorifies God.

Thinking back to the example of the Lord's Prayer, we remember the words "your will be done, on earth as it is in heaven" (Matthew 6:10 ESV). Our prayer is a verbal act of obedience to surrender our desires and agendas, recognizing that God's plans and purposes are far greater and more perfect than our own.

So, since prayer is an act of obedience, we should pray faithfully, whether we feel like it or not. We shouldn't wait for the perfect moment or the right emotions before coming to God. It is always the right moment to pray, because it's always the right time to obey.

Let's make prayer a daily habit and watch as He transforms our hearts.

Think About It

- Why is it important to align our will to God's will?
- Can you think of a time when praying about something changed your mind about it?
- What prevents you from praying faithfully?

Pray About It

- Stop and pray today at different times—whether or not you feel like it.
- Talk to God about what gets in the way of praying more often.
- Ask God to help you obey.

....

Lord, I admit that I need Your help in this journey of obedient prayer. My own desires and distractions often get in the way. Please help me do what's right.

38.
Search and Find

"You will look for Me and find Me,
when you look for Me with all your heart."
JEREMIAH 29:13

Ever wish you could get closer to God—close enough to be certain of His presence in your life? In moments of deep sadness or during a long sleepless night or in the middle of a difficult trial, you may wish you could feel a tangible connection with Him—to know He's close enough that you could reach out and touch Him or hear His voice.

In reality, you *can* feel this level of closeness with Him if you learn to meet Him consistently in prayer. When you talk to Him regularly and transparently—not merely out of duty or obligation—you will begin to sense His closeness. You will know He's there even if you can't hold His hand or hear Him speak.

In a letter the prophet Jeremiah wrote to the Israelites while they were in exile, he recorded something that applies to us too. He wrote, "You will look for [God] and find [Him], when you look for [Him] with all your heart."

If you want to find God, search for Him with all your heart. And that begins with talking to Him in prayer.

Think About It

- Do you wish you could be closer to God?

- Are there times you feel like God is far away?

- Why do you think God waits for you to search for Him in order for Him to be found?

Pray About It

- Tell God how close you'd like to be to Him.

- Ask for wisdom to know how to search with your whole heart.

- Thank Him for the promise that He will be found.

....

God, help me to seek You with all my heart,
with an honest and undivided devotion.

39.
What Are You Saying?

"When you pray, do not be as those who pretend to be someone they are not. They love to stand and pray in the places of worship or in the streets so people can see them. For sure, I tell you, they have all the reward they are going to get."

MATTHEW 6:5

Have you ever been intimidated to pray in front of somebody? Maybe you've thought, *What if I say something silly?* or *That person prays so much better than I do.*

Sometimes we get caught up in thinking we need to use eloquent words or fancy phrases when we pray. But here's the thing: prayer isn't about impressing anybody—it's about talking to God with a sincere heart.

God doesn't need us to impress Him with poetic prayers. In fact, we *can't* impress Him, because anything we're able to do that's good comes from Him anyway. Even our words come from a mind and heart that He created.

God is most interested in the heart behind our words. Do we really mean what we're praying? Are we trying to please God or people? Are we being fake or sincere? Who are we actually talking to when we pray? Matthew 6:5 says, "When you pray, do not be as those who pretend to be someone they are not."

So say what you mean and mean what you say.

Think About It

- Do you try to impress other people when you pray?
- How comfortable are you praying in front of people?
- When you pray, how do you keep your attention on God?

Pray About It

- Ask God for the courage to be honest and vulnerable when you talk to Him.
- Ask God to help you focus on the substance rather than the eloquence of your prayers.
- Thank God for His invitation to talk to Him without any pressure of performance.

. . . .

Father, I come to You with a humble heart,
desiring to be sincere in my prayers to You.

40.
Give and Take

Give all your cares to the Lord and He will give you strength.
He will never let those who are right with Him be shaken.
PSALM 55:22

Life can get pretty intense, can't it? Between school, friends, family, and everything else you're juggling, it's easy to start feeling like you're carrying many heavy burdens on your shoulders.

It's absolutely normal to have burdens—we all do. But you don't have to carry them all by yourself. In fact, God doesn't *want* you to carry them alone. He wants you to give those burdens to Him.

Have you ever watched or played volleyball? During a game, the players quickly "volley" the ball back and forth. As soon as they receive the ball, they send it back. What if we did the same with our burdens? Face something difficult—send it to God. Face something else difficult—send it to God, as well.

Tell God what's on your mind and what's weighing down your heart and mind. Ask God for guidance, peace, and strength. Sometimes the simple act of telling God about what's happening in your life can make the burdens feel lighter.

Psalm 55:22 tells us that when we give our burdens to the Lord, He will give us His strength. That's a great trade!

Think About It

- Have you ever experienced a situation or burden that felt too heavy to carry on your own?

- Do you truly believe God can help you with your burdens?

- What is weighing down your heart and mind today?

Pray About It

- Tell God about anything heavy you are carrying today.

- Ask God to trade His strength for your burdens.

- Thank God for His help.

. . . .

Lord, thank You for the promise that I don't have to carry these heavy burdens on my own. You are a good and gracious God to carry them for me.

41.
Noble Beginnings

Then we will not turn away from You. Give us new life again, and we will call on Your name.
PSALM 80:18

In recent years, Christian groups around the United States have reported stories of spiritual revival happening on college campuses. Even just the possibility of widespread revival happening in America is hopeful and exciting.

Remember that revival, a topic we looked at earlier in this book, is often a collective awakening of hearts. A church or Christian community comes together in prayer, seeking God's presence, hearing from God's Word, and obeying God's commands. In the words of Psalm 80:18, revival is God giving us new life again.

Christian revival—whether in a community or an individual heart—is life-changing because it involves turning from sin, surrendering to God, and committing to Christlikeness.

Revival is something we should always want. Revival indicates people are getting right with God, and that is always good.

But it doesn't need to be a grand, public event in order to be powerful or transformative. Revival can happen in the heart of a believer during small, ordinary moments of prayer too.

Big or little, it all starts with prayer.

Think About It

- Do you ever pray for revival in your own heart or in the church?

- Do you believe widespread revival can happen today? Why or why not?

- Why is revival impossible without prayer?

Pray About It

- Ask God to do revival work in your heart.

- Ask God to do revival work in the church.

- Thank Him for the ways He brought revival throughout history.

Lord, please bring revival to places where hope seems distant, and let the gospel light shine in the darkest corners of the world.

42.
There's No Need

*And my God will give you everything you need
because of His great riches in Christ Jesus.*
PHILIPPIANS 4:19

Where do you go when you really, *really* need something? Do you talk to your parents? Do you chat with your friends? Do you keep the need hidden because you hate asking for help?

God wants us to bring every need to Him. Prayer is where we lay it all out, trusting that God is listening, that He cares, and that He's ready to give us exactly what we need, sometimes even more than we could imagine.

God, in His abundant kindness, invites us to bring everything to Him—our big needs, our small needs, our messy needs. He isn't intimidated by our struggles or put off by our asking. Even if He has to say no to our request, it's because He understands something we don't know, and He loves us too much to give us something that will ultimately harm us.

Here's something important to remember: In the midst of our crazy, beautiful lives, what we actually need most is not a quick fix or an easy solution to a current problem. What we need most is God Himself.

God is the answer to every need we have.

Think About It

- What do you need in your life right now?

- Do you believe there is anything God can't provide for you?

- Can you remember a time you prayed for something you needed and the answer wasn't what you expected?

Pray About It

- Thank God for the invitation to bring your needs to Him.

- Tell God anything you currently need in your life.

- Trust God to meet the need—and to be the greatest answer to every need you have.

....

Father, I come before You with gratitude for the promise that You are my provider. You know the needs of my heart and life, so I lay those needs before You, trusting that Your answer will be perfect.

43.
Grace Notes

Let yourself be brought low before the Lord.
Then He will lift you up and help you.
JAMES 4:10

Prayer is our daily reminder that we are in desperate need of God's grace. Without prayer, we might wrongly believe we can handle life on our own.

Imagine you're going about your day, juggling a long to-do list of homework and chores and practice, and suddenly you think, *I'm overwhelmed! I can't do all of this on my own. I need help!* And so, you stop and pray about it. You ask God to give you the strength to do all the things you need to get done.

That's actually grace. It is kind of God to remind us that we need Him.

And you know what? It pleases God when we ask Him for His help. Every bit of chaos in our lives exists to remind us that we are not God but that we have access to Him through prayer. And He wants to meet us there.

Prayer is where we get to experience God's grace firsthand. It's more than a reminder of our need; it's the very place where God meets us with open arms. It's where we find forgiveness for our failures and strength for our weakness. God delights to give us grace when we pray.

Next time you're overwhelmed, run to God.

Think About It

- Do you pray when you're overwhelmed?
- How does prayer grow humility in your heart?
- Do you believe God wants to help you?

Pray About It

- Thank God for His gift of grace.
- Thank God for reminding you that you need Him.
- Tell God about anything currently overwhelming you.

....

Lord, thank You for Your immeasurable gift of grace, made possible through Jesus. Thank You for making that grace available to me when I need it.

44.
Build Each Other Up

A man cannot please God unless he has faith.
Anyone who comes to God must believe that He is.
That one must also know that God gives what is
promised to the one who keeps on looking for Him.
HEBREWS 11:6

Have you ever heard the expression "Actions speak louder than words"? In a world that is oversaturated with talk, this age-old proverb serves as a reminder that words are cheap without the right actions to back them up. It suggests that our beliefs are more accurately reflected in how we *act* than in what we *say*.

Most Christians would acknowledge that they believe God can do anything. But considering how few Christians actually pray with any consistency, it would seem not many Christians believe it enough to ask God for help when they need it.

Hebrews 11:6 tells us that we cannot please God unless we have faith. And it isn't enough to *say* we have faith; we need to back up our words with actions that demonstrate we have faith.

Prayer is an expression of our faith in God's power.

Prayer is an action that pleases God and speaks louder than empty words.

Think About It

- How does prayer go beyond just expressing words and become a demonstration of faith in God's power?

- Can you think of a time you prayed for something that felt impossible and saw God answer your request?

- How has your faith deepened as a result of prayer?

Pray About It

- Tell God what you believe about His power in your life.

- Ask God for courage to be faithful in backing up your words with actions.

- Thank God for the ability to try again when we fail to pray as we should.

....

Lord, please forgive me for the times my words and actions haven't matched. Please strengthen my faith and help my choices to reflect my trust in You every day.

45.
By All Accounts

Make a clean heart in me, O God. Give me
a new spirit that will not be moved.
Psalm 51:10

We've talked previously in this book about how prayer is our way to seek forgiveness and reconciliation with our heavenly Father. Now let's build on that idea: Prayer is specifically the way we handle our sin quickly so that we can maintain fellowship with our heavenly Father. It's how we keep short acounts with Him. The idea of keeping short accounts with God means we regularly and promptly acknowledge our sins before Him.

We know that repentance isn't just a half-hearted apology or a casual acknowledgment of a mistake. True repentance is an honest recognition of our sin as rebellion against a holy God. It isn't fun and it isn't comfortable, but it's good and right.

During your day, if you know you've sinned—in your words, your actions, or your attitudes—stop and address it right then and there with God in prayer. It doesn't need to be a formal or fancy prayer. Simply tell Him what you've done and how you are sorry. Ask Him to forgive you and help you change.

When we repent, we're essentially saying, "I don't want this sin; I want Christ above all else." And that brings God glory.

Think About It

- Are you quick to repent when you know you've sinned?

- Why is repentance sometimes difficult to do?

- Why do you believe it brings God glory when we repent?

Pray About It

- Ask God to search your heart and show you anything you need to acknowledge to Him.

- Repent of any sin God brings to your mind.

- Pray for the strength to say what needs to be said.

. . . .

Father, thank You for the gentle nudging of Your Spirit that reveals the areas in my life where I fall short, where I have strayed from Your perfect standard.

46.
Escape!

You have never been tempted to sin in any different way than other people. God is faithful. He will not allow you to be tempted more than you can take. But when you are tempted, He will make a way for you to keep from falling into sin.
1 CORINTHIANS 10:13

By now as a Christian you probably know that much of life is basically a tug-of-war between doing what you know is right and giving in to temptations—large and small—that grab your attention at the most inconvenient times.

Maybe these temptations include making poor choices to fit in with a crowd, lowering your values to gain acceptance, or even being dishonest with your friends or parents in order to keep people happy.

The struggle is real, and unfortunately, temptation doesn't magically disappear by simply getting older. It's lifelong. But here's a welcome truth: You don't have to handle the temptation alone. God is with you, and in the words of 1 Corinthians 10:13, "He will make a way for you to keep from falling into sin." *He has given you prayer.*

In those moments when it feels like you're standing at the edge of a cliff, ready to take a nosedive into bad choices, pray. God wants to help you, and prayer is far more powerful than your willpower.

Think About It

- What do you do to fight temptation in your life? Do you pray when you're tempted?

- Why do you believe prayer is a powerful tool in the fight with sin?

- Do you believe prayer can really make a difference?

Pray About It

- Ask God to help you fight temptation with prayer.

- Tell God about any consistent, repeating temptations in your life.

- Thank God for His love, compassion, and willingness to help.

....

Thank You, Lord, for Your promise that I don't have to face temptation alone. Thank You for giving me access to You through prayer any time I need it.

47.
On Top of the World

Go into His gates giving thanks and into His holy place with praise. Give thanks to Him. Honor His name.

PSALM 100:4

Have you ever noticed that when you talk to God in prayer, you start feeling more grateful? When you pour out your heart to God, something shifts. It's difficult to put a finger on it, but it's like a perspective upgrade.

Prayer causes us to slow down and notice things: There is beauty in the mundane and blessings in the chaos. God has been faithful in the past and will be faithful in the future....

Prayer cultivates gratitude. It isn't the primary reason we pray—we pray because it glorifies God—but a grateful heart pleases Him too. Building a habit of prayer opens our eyes to the richness of life and deepens our awareness of God's goodness all around us.

Psalm 100 encourages us to give thanks to God, and verse 5 explains why: "For the Lord is good. His loving-kindness lasts forever. And He is faithful to all people and to all their children-to-come." God has been faithful to you. His goodness to you isn't fleeting or distant. It's a rock-solid reality, absolutely consistent regardless of the ever-shifting landscape of your life.

Doesn't just reading those words make you feel a little lighter?

Think About It

- What can you be grateful to God for today?
- Do you find that prayer generally makes you more grateful?
- Besides prayer, what other ways can you show gratitude to God?

Pray About It

- Thank God for three specific things.
- Ask God to give you a heart of gratitude.
- Praise God for His goodness and faithfulness.

- -

Lord, thank You for the breath in my lungs, for the beating of my heart—for the gift of life itself. Your mercies are new every morning, and for that, I am truly thankful.

48.
Keep Going!

You must keep praying. Keep watching! Be thankful always.
COLOSSIANS 4:2

By now you're probably getting the idea that prayer is a marathon and not a sprint. Being faithful in prayer is about sticking with it even when you don't feel like praying, when you don't get the answers you want to your requests, or when you don't feel like you have the right words. Prayer is about faithfully and gratefully showing up in God's presence because you love Him and want to honor Him, regardless of how you feel. Sometimes—maybe even *often*—faithful prayer requires us to push through distractions and doubts.

Remember this: Your greatest enemy, the devil, doesn't want you to pray. He would rather see you mindlessly scrolling social media or worrying about what people think of you or bingeing a show instead of talking to God. *Why?* Because prayer is powerful, and because connecting with God is the wisest use of your time.

So, when you feel that normal resistance to pray—when suddenly anything seems more enticing than spending quiet time with God—understand what's happening.

And choose to pray anyway.

Think About It

- Have you ever wanted to give up on prayer? What motivated you to continue?

- What would persevering in prayer look like in your life?

- What are your most frequent distractions from prayer?

Pray About It

- Tell God why prayer can be difficult for you at times.

- Ask God to help you become persistent in prayer.

- Thank God for giving you something as powerful as connection with Him.

....

God, please give me the strength and discipline to be more persistent in praying. Help me overcome the doubts and distractions that keep me from following You fully. Teach me to wait patiently for Your perfect answers, and tune my heart to Your perfect timing.

49.
On Worship and Wonder

Give to the Lord, O sons of the powerful. Give to the Lord shining-greatness and strength. Give to the Lord the honor that belongs to Him. Worship the Lord in the beauty of holy living.

<small>PSALM 29:1–2</small>

Prayer gives us the opportunity to express our love and adoration for God and His attributes. Certainly, we can do this when we sing or play music, but prayer gives us the chance to tell God in our own words what we most appreciate about Him.

What do you love most about God? Stop and consider the sheer magnitude of His love for you, expressed through the sacrifice of His only Son, Jesus. Or consider His grace that draws you into relationship with Him, not based on anything good you've done, but based entirely on His goodness toward you. Or what about His unchanging character? He is faithful to you through every season. What a profound comfort to know He will never ever change regardless of whether everything else in the world does.

His sovereignty that governs, His grace that saves, His mercy that forgives, and His faithfulness that endures— we have so much to praise God for. And those are just a few examples.

What can you praise Him for today?

Think About It

- What is one of your favorite attributes of God?

- In your prayers, how often do you praise God for what He means to you?

- How can praising God for His attributes change the way you think about your requests?

Pray About It

- Praise God for at least three things you appreciate about Him.

- Ask God to help you love Him more.

- Thank God for a specific way you see His character at work in your life.

....

Thank You, God, for who You are. You are truly the same yesterday, today, and forever (Hebrews 13:8), and I am grateful.

50.
Asking for a Friend

If you do not have wisdom, ask God for it. He is always ready to give it to you and will never say you are wrong for asking.
JAMES 1:5

In prayer, we have the incredible privilege of laying our doubts and questions at the feet of God Himself.

You know those pesky questions that nag at the corners of your mind when you read a passage out of the Bible or listen to a sermon? Or you know those doubts you have about some aspect of your life or faith when you're lying awake in bed at night? Or maybe something you've been taught doesn't quite line up with something you've experienced. God *wants* you to bring those doubts and questions to Him.

You don't need to pretend you have everything figured out. Doubts and questions aren't something to be afraid of bringing to God. Doubts and questions actually illustrate that we're trying to understand truth. Apathy—a lack of concern—is far more dangerous than our doubts and questions.

When we lay our doubts or questions at the feet of God in prayer, we demonstrate humility. We acknowledge the limitations of our understanding while recognizing the infinite wisdom and sovereignty of our Creator.

Have a question? Ask God.

Think About It

- How comfortable are you bringing your doubts and questions to God in prayer?

- How do you think bringing your doubts and questions to God could actually strengthen your relationship with Him?

- Why is God the safest person to talk to about your questions?

Pray About It

- Thank God for the invitation to talk to Him about anything.

- Ask for the courage to always be honest with Him.

- Talk to Him about any questions or doubts you currently have.

....

Lord, I thank You for inviting me to lay my doubts before You. I know You hold the answers to all things, so I'm grateful that You also hold my questions with tenderness and kindness.

51.
Garden Conversation

*So if you eat or drink or whatever you
do, do everything to honor God.*
1 CORINTHIANS 10:31

On the night before Jesus was crucified, He went to the garden of Gethsemane. The air thick with tension, Jesus fully aware of what was coming, He began to pray: "Father, if it can be done, take away what must happen to Me. Even so, not what I want, but what You want" (Luke 22:42).

In His darkest hours, Jesus didn't shy away from God; He pressed in, spoke honestly, and sought God's glory in all things. His prayer was a raw and honest plea for the deep desire of His heart, but even as He asked His Father to make a way for Him to avoid what was coming, He surrendered His will to God.

Prayer is also our opportunity to seek God's glory in all things.

As Jesus showed in the garden, we *should* ask God for the deep desires of our hearts while also maintaining an attitude of surrender. There is profound wisdom in confidently asking while also humbly yielding to God's will.

Jesus showed us how to do it.

Think About It

- How is seeking God's glory in prayer different from simply listing prayer requests?

- What does Jesus' prayer in the garden teach us about how we're invited to pray?

- God ultimately said no to Jesus' request to avoid crucifixion. What can this fact teach us about God's no to our requests?

Pray About It

- Ask God for the deep desires of your heart.

- Submit to God's will, telling Him you want to seek His glory above your own desires.

- Ask God for the courage to persistently seek His glory, even in the face of challenges and disappointments.

....

Lord, in all things, I want to seek Your glory above everything, acknowledging Your sovereignty and trusting in Your wisdom.

52.
The Daily Grind

Teach me Your way, O Lord. I will walk in Your truth. May my heart fear Your name.
PSALM 86:11

We've discussed a few times in this book that prayer is much more than a mere ritual or a checkbox on our spiritual to-do list. But why does it matter? Is it really that big of a deal to view prayer as a task instead of a relationship?

When we approach prayer with the attitude that it is a duty, not an invitation, we risk falling into the trap of going through the motions without engaging our hearts. When we view prayer like we do a homework assignment that we "just need to get done," we miss the opportunity to pour out our deepest concerns, joys, and confessions before God, who listens and cares.

Prayer is ultimately about cultivating a relationship with the God who loves you beyond measure. It was never meant to become one more burden in your already overpacked day.

Don't settle for a mechanical approach to prayer. Come before God with a genuine desire to talk to Him—that's far better than any checklist or ritual.

Think About It

- Have you ever viewed prayer as something to check off a list? Did it impact how you prayed?

- Is it easy or challenging for you to be authentic with God in prayer?

- How would viewing prayer as a means to relationship with God change the way you talked to Him?

Pray About It

- Thank God for the privilege of building a relationship with Him.

- Tell God any of the reasons why prayer is difficult or challenging.

- Ask God for help to view prayer as a gift.

....

Thank You for being a God who listens, a God who cares, and a God who desires a relationship with me.

53.
Heart of the Matter

"Look to the Lord and ask for His strength.
Look to Him all the time."
1 CHRONICLES 16:11

Prayer is the heartbeat of the Christian life—the rhythm that pulses through every day and every decision. Have a need? Talk to God. Afraid of the future? Talk to God. Grateful for something? Talk to God.

In many ways, your actual physical heartbeat and your prayer life are similar. For example. . .

Generally speaking, *your heartbeat should be steady and consistent.* So, too, your prayer life shouldn't happen in fits and spurts but should be the slow and steady drumbeat of your daily walk with God. *Your heartbeat isn't optional;* you absolutely need it to live. So, too, your prayer life shouldn't be take-it-or-leave-it—it should be the core of your relationship with God. *Your heartbeat helps doctors determine your overall health.* So, too, your prayer life helps signify the health and vitality of your spiritual life—revealing the strength of your love for, trust in, and reliance on God.

Strengthen your heart; strengthen your health.

Strengthen your prayer life; strengthen your walk with God. Your heartbeat and your prayer habits are *life*.

Think About It

- What are some simple things you can do to strengthen your prayer life?
- Since your prayer life is a good indicator of your spiritual health, how are you doing spiritually right now?
- Can you think of anyone in your life who demonstrates a healthy prayer life?

Pray About It

- Ask God for a deep and genuine desire to prioritize prayer.
- Ask God for a renewed passion to talk to Him.
- Ask God to reveal areas of your life where you have neglected to involve Him in daily decisions.

....

Lord, please give me the discipline to prioritize prayer in the midst of life's busyness. Help my days to be marked by intentional moments of communion with You.

54.
Just Be Honest

*Hannah was very troubled. She prayed to
the Lord and cried with sorrow.*
1 SAMUEL 1:10

In 1 Samuel 1, we read the story of Hannah and how she prayed unapologetically to the Lord for the desire of her heart. Hannah wanted a baby, "but the Lord had made it so she could not have children" (1 Samuel 1:5). So Hannah decided to make a promise to the Lord. She committed in prayer that if God would give her a son, she would dedicate him to the Lord.

Hannah didn't hold back; she was honest with God—no filters, no pretense. She was so passionate in her praying that when Eli the priest saw her, he assumed she was drunk. When he confronted her about this, Hannah responded, "No. . . I am a woman troubled in spirit. I have not drunk wine or strong drink, but I was pouring out my soul to the Lord" (1 Samuel 1:15).

Do you need to pour out your soul to the Lord? God knows what is in your heart and He's waiting for you to have the courage to be truthful with Him about it.

Take a page from Hannah's story and speak honestly with your heavenly Father about anything troubling you today.

Think About It

- Do you have an unfulfilled desire in your heart that you need to bring to God in prayer?

- How does Hannah's approach to prayer encourage you as you pray?

- How does Hannah's prayer demonstrate trust and faith in God?

Pray About It

- Like Hannah did, pour out your soul to the Lord.

- Ask God to give you patience, faith, and trust— just as He gave Hannah.

- Thank God for hearing you when you pray.

....

Lord, thank You for Hannah's example—a reminder that I can bring my deepest desires, struggles, and joys to You without fear or reservation.

55.
Word to the Wise

I have called to You, O God, for You will answer
me. Listen to me and hear my words.

PSALM 17:6

Prayer is not a monologue but a dialogue—a conversation where speaking is only one part and listening is equally important.

Maybe you're thinking, *But I've never heard God speak!* Many—if not most—Christians throughout history would say the same thing. This is where God's Word becomes especially important when discussing God's answers to our prayers. Throughout history, God has preferred to communicate in writing through the pages of scripture. Through the Bible, God speaks to every generation and every heart that seeks Him: "God's Word is living and powerful" (Hebrews 4:12). It is just as personal and relevant today as it was when the words were written.

God also speaks to us through the counsel of godly people. In a group of wise counselors, there is safety (Proverbs 11:14).

Think about the Psalms. David, a man after God's own heart, poured out his soul in prayer, but he also listened. He waited on God, sought godly counsel, and acknowledged his need for guidance, confident that God would answer him.

Like David, we should pray with an eager anticipation that God will respond.

Think About It

- Have you ever experienced a situation where you found answers to your prayers in God's Word?

- How do you think prayer and Bible reading work together?

- How do you listen for an answer after you talk to God in prayer?

Pray About It

- Thank God for the gift of His Word.

- Pick a verse (or set of verses) in Psalms and pray those words to the Lord.

- Ask God to help you listen for what you need to hear.

. . . .

Thank You, Lord, for the assurance that when I call on You in prayer, You incline Your ear to listen. Thank You, also, for the answers You provide.

56.
For Goodness' Sake

"O give thanks to the Lord, for He is good.
His loving-kindness lasts forever."
1 Chronicles 16:34

Prayer is a bold declaration that God is good in *every* circumstance. This declaration isn't naive optimism that ignores life's painful realities. Life is hard—there's no question about it. Our confidence in God's goodness has nothing to do with circumstances. It's an unwavering trust in the character of God.

God is good when we *receive* the answer we want to the prayer we offer.

God is good when we *don't receive* the answer we want to the prayer we offer.

God is good, even when our prayers feel like they're met with silence.

God is good, period.

That kind of logic doesn't make sense in a world where someone's goodness is contingent on what she has to offer. But to a child of God, we know God's goodness doesn't hinge on the outcomes of our prayers; it's the essence of who He is.

So in every prayer and with every request, we can say with the psalmist, "You are good and You do good" (Psalm 119:68).

And we can trust that it is true.

Think About It

- How is your understanding of God's goodness influenced by whether your prayers are answered?

- Do you still believe God is good when you don't get the answers you request?

- How does the idea of God's goodness provide comfort to you when you are disappointed by life?

Pray About It

- Thank God for His goodness.

- Tell God you trust Him, even when you don't get the answers you desire.

- Tell God what you need.

....

God, please forgive me for the times I've questioned Your goodness in the face of unanswered prayers or challenging circumstances. Today, I choose to anchor my faith in the unshakable truth that You are good and do only good.

57.
You Have Been Commissioned

*Then He said to His followers, "There is much grain
ready to gather. But the workmen are few. Pray then
to the Lord Who is the Owner of the grain fields that
He will send workmen to gather His grain."*
MATTHEW 9:37–38

Right before Jesus returned to heaven after His crucifixion
and resurrection, He shared this instruction with His disciples:
"Go and make followers of all the nations" (Matthew 28:19).
Jesus' words have become known as the Great Commission—
His command to take the gospel to every nook and cranny
of this world until every person has heard the good news
that Jesus saves.

One way we obey this command? We pray for the gospel
to spread.

If Jesus were giving the Great Commission to us today,
He would likely urge us to move beyond our self-centered
prayers to prayers that echo the concerns of God's heart for
every people group on earth. When was the last time you
prayed for unbelieving people groups around the world?
When was the last time you were burdened for unbelievers
to trust Christ?

Praying for lost people mirrors the heart of God.

Our prayers should extend beyond the borders of our own lives to include people here and around the world who do not yet know that Jesus loves them and died to save them.

What an incredible privilege to share this truth.

Think About It

- Do you pray with a global perspective?
- Who do you know that still needs to trust Jesus?
- How much difference do you think prayer can make for lost people?

Pray About It

- Pray for someone who needs to be saved.
- Ask God to give you a bigger love for the world.
- Find a map of the world and pray for different countries by name.

Lord, please open my eyes to see the nations as You see them, each person a precious creation who needs to know about Your redeeming love.

58.
Mean Girls

Pray and give thanks for those who make trouble for you.
Yes, pray for them instead of talking against them.
ROMANS 12:14

In Romans 12:14, Paul gave us a very uncomfortable command when he wrote, "Pray and give thanks for those who make trouble for you." Another way of saying it: When someone's giving you a hard time, don't get upset about it or vent to your friends. Instead, pray for that person.

This command is a hard pill to swallow. This response to troublemakers is not our default setting. Most of us would at least prefer to roll our eyes or throw some shade their way. But what if Paul's command—which is ultimately God's command since He inspired Paul to write the words in Romans—is less about changing the person making trouble and more about transforming *us*?

God never commands us to pretend everything is fine. He doesn't ask us to pretend that our feelings haven't been hurt or that our day hasn't been disrupted by someone else's selfishness. Instead, we're free to acknowledge the struggle and then invite God into the mess.

When we pray for people who make trouble for us, we're surrendering them and the details of the situation to God, who has power to change hearts and fix circumstances.

And isn't that what we should want most?

Think About It

- Do you find it challenging to pray for people who are unkind to you? Why or why not?

- Why do you think God wants us to pray for people who are difficult?

- Which do you think has the better long-term outcome: seeking revenge or stopping to pray?

Pray About It

- Ask for help in learning to pray for difficult people.

- Admit that it's sometimes hard to do.

- Talk to God about anyone in your life who is currently causing you trouble.

....

God, please help me learn to see people through Your eyes, recognizing the brokenness that might be driving their unkind actions.

59.
When to Quit

Let us keep looking to Jesus. Our faith comes from Him and He is the One Who makes it perfect. He did not give up when He had to suffer shame and die on a cross. He knew of the joy that would be His later. Now He is sitting at the right side of God.

HEBREWS 12:2

We've talked previously in this book about the importance of persevering in prayer. But prayer is also the key to persevering in life.

Perseverance is the steadfast persistence and determination to continue moving forward despite difficulties, obstacles, or discouragement. It involves enduring through challenges, setbacks, and adversity. It requires a combination of commitment to the goal and reliance on God's strength.

Hebrews 12:1 says, "Let us put every thing out of our lives that keeps us from doing what we should. Let us keep running in the race that God has planned for us." This is perseverance.

The next verse answers the question of how we persevere: "Let us keep looking to Jesus" (Hebrews 12:2). If you rely on your own strength, eventually you will get tired. If you rely on your own wisdom, eventually you will find its limitations.

If you rely on your own resources, eventually you will come up short of what you need. But if you rely on God, you will have everything you need.

When should you quit doing what God wants you to do? Never.

Think About It

- Why is it hard to persevere?

- Do you believe perseverance comes naturally to human beings, or do you think perseverance is something we have to learn?

- Can you think of a time you kept doing right even though life was challenging?

Pray About It

- Ask God to give you strength to persevere.

- Thank God for the example of Jesus, who persevered when life was hard.

- Tell God why you want to be faithful to Him no matter what happens.

....

God, help me to remember that Your love and power are greater than any obstacle I will ever encounter.

60.
Disaster Relief

The news about Jesus went out all the more. Many people
came to hear Him and to be healed of their diseases.
Then He went away by Himself to pray in a desert.
LUKE 5:15–16

Sometimes life can feel a little out of control, can't it?
Sometimes the demands on our time—school, homework,
tests, practices, rehearsals—can start to overwhelm us. Or
maybe our relationships can lead us to feel like life is falling
apart. Maybe somebody at school is being unkind or gossiping
about you, or maybe you and your friend just had a big misunderstanding. Or maybe many good things are happening
at once and life feels intense in a good way.

Prayer is where we find peace amid the chaos.

Throughout the Gospels, we see moments when Jesus—
after healing the sick, feeding the multitudes, or preaching
hard truths to big crowds—would slip away into the wil-
derness to pray. He demonstrated God's desire for us. Jesus
often chose prayer over the drama of people.

When we pray, we aren't commanded to pretend the
chaos doesn't exist. Instead—with arms open wide—God

invites us to bring it all to Him. There is nothing too messy, too chaotic, or too tangled up for God to handle.

Think About It

- When life is challenging, is it easier or harder for you to pray?

- Why do you think God wants you to pray when you are overwhelmed?

- How do you create a space for prayer in a busy or big day?

Pray About It

- Thank God for the invitation to come to Him at any time and in any place.

- Talk to God about anything chaotic in your life right now.

- Ask God to give you courage to choose prayer throughout the day.

....

Father, in the middle of life's whirlwinds, help me find my quiet place of refuge in Your presence.

61.
No Laughing Matter

*When Daniel knew that the king had written his name
on this law, he went into his house where, in his upper
room, he had windows open toward Jerusalem. There
he got down on his knees three times each day, praying
and giving thanks to his God, as he had done before.*

DANIEL 6:10

We should take prayer as seriously as Daniel did when he
lived in Babylon.

Remember, Daniel lived as a captive in a land filled with
idol worship. But he protected his heart from false gods and
remained completely faithful to God in prayer. In fact, when
evil men came to report Daniel to the king in order to get
him in trouble, their biggest complaint about him was "He is
still asking things of his God three times a day" (Daniel 6:13).

Because Daniel refused to worship the king and instead
prayed to the true and living God, Daniel was sentenced to
death and thrown into the lions' den. You probably know what
happened next. God shut the lions' mouths and protected
Daniel's life.

Today, your world is filled with idols and opportunities
to worship false gods. They're not the same false gods that

existed in Babylon all those years ago, but the temptations are just as real. Daniel's faithful example to pray should remind us to keep our hearts turned toward the God who is faithful and true.

Think About It

- What do you believe motivated Daniel to keep praying in Babylon?

- What did Daniel's decision to keep praying reveal about his priorities?

- How is Daniel's commitment to prayer a good example for us today?

Pray About It

- Talk to God about how you want to take prayer seriously.

- Thank God for the good example of Daniel in the Bible.

- Praise God for the way He loves and protects His people.

Lord, please help me be faithful to pray. I want to talk to You throughout my day, just like Daniel did.

62.
First Responder

The prayer given in faith will heal the sick man, and the Lord will raise him up. If he has sinned, he will be forgiven.
JAMES 5:15

Prayer is where we go for healing—physical, emotional, and spiritual. God is the Great Physician and the ultimate healer. There is nothing and nobody that He cannot heal. The Bible tells us that we should pray for healing—with big faith and big expectations in what God can do.

Sometimes we don't ask for healing because it seems impossible. Maybe somebody we love is really sick and it doesn't look like healing will happen. Or sometimes we don't ask for healing because we're afraid to get our hopes up and then be disappointed. What if God chooses to say no? That's a hard question to consider.

When we pray for healing—either for ourselves or for someone else—we're expressing our trust in God, who is both compassionate and capable. It's our way of saying, "God, I know You can provide healing, and so I'm trusting You to do it if it's Your will."

It's important to understand that if God says no to your request for healing, it isn't because you prayed incorrectly or didn't have enough faith. Sometimes God's plans are different from ours, and those plans are always for our good.

But He always invites us to *ask*.

Think About It

- Have you ever prayed to God for healing?
- What challenges or questions arise when you think about praying for healing?
- Is there anyone in your life who needs God's healing today?

Pray About It

- Pray about someone who needs healing.
- Thank God, the Great Physician, for the invitation to ask for healing.
- Ask God to strengthen your faith in His ability to heal.

Thank You, Lord, for Your role as the Great Physician. You provide healing in ways I never even know or understand. Help me to learn to ask for healing when needed.

63.
Justice Delayed Is Not Justice Denied

For the Lord loves what is fair and right. He does not leave the people alone who belong to Him. They are kept forever. But the children of the sinful will be cut off.

Psalm 37:28

Truth be told, this world can be a dark and difficult place, and it's okay to acknowledge that. When sin entered the garden of Eden, everything changed.

One of the ongoing consequences of life in this fallen and broken post-Eden world is that injustice is real. Turn on the news, scroll through social media, or simply walk through a local store and you'll likely see and hear things that shouldn't be seen or heard.

But even though the world is filled with evil, you *can* be part of the solution. God wants you to pray about the injustice you see.

Never underestimate that God cares about what's happening in the world. The psalmist said, "For the Lord loves what is fair and right." Isn't that helpful to know? We do not serve a God who is mean or irrational. He doesn't stand in heaven eagerly rubbing His hands together, waiting to watch the world fall apart. No, Exodus 34:6 describes God as filled with loving-pity and loving-favor, slow to get angry, and filled with loving-kindness and truth.

Our God loves justice and will someday make everything right again.

Think About It

- In what ways should injustice motivate you to pray?

- What do you think happens when you talk to God about the injustice you see?

- How does knowing that God is good give you hope for the world?

Pray About It

- Praise God for loving what is fair and right.

- Ask God to help people who are being mistreated.

- Ask God for opportunities to be a gospel witness in this dark world.

Lord, keep my heart fixed on You, trusting that
Your justice will prevail in the world.

64.
Decisions, Decisions

Show me Your ways, O Lord. Teach me Your paths.
Lead me in Your truth and teach me. For You are the
God Who saves me. I wait for You all day long.
PSALM 25:4–5

Life is filled with decisions, isn't it? From big choices that could shape your entire future to those small, everyday decisions that you make without thinking much about them, they all have consequences—good or bad—and they can start to feel like a lot.

Sometimes it's easier to remember to pray about the big, life-altering choices than it is to remember all those day-to-day decisions. *But God welcomes your prayer for every issue.*

And even better, God *wants* you to have the wisdom you need. You see only what's right in front of you, but God sees your whole life—past, present, and future—from every angle. So it makes sense that you go to Him when you have a question about what you should do next.

Praying about every decision doesn't make life easy, but it does give us the confidence that we aren't navigating life blindly. God is a trustworthy captain who is committed to taking us where we're meant to go. He knows the destination, the purpose, and the plans He has for us.

And those plans are always and only good.

Think About It

- Is it your habit to talk to God before you make decisions?

- Do you find it easier to talk to Him about the big or the small decisions? Why?

- Do you truly believe God's plans for you are good?

Pray About It

- Spend time talking to God about decisions you are making in your life right now.

- Tell God any concerns you have for the future.

- Ask God for wisdom.

....

Heavenly Father, thank You for being with me in every decision, big or small. Help me to remember to talk to You about my choices.

65.
Down-to-Earth

So put away all pride from yourselves. You are standing under the powerful hand of God. At the right time He will lift you up. Give all your worries to Him because He cares for you.
1 PETER 5:6–7

We've talked earlier in this book about how prayer *requires* humility, but prayer also *demonstrates* humility. The only type of prayer that pleases God is a humble prayer.

When we pray in a way that honors God—no matter what we choose to talk to Him about—two specific things are happening that demonstrate humility.

First, we're acknowledging a need. When we talk to God, we tell Him about the challenges and circumstances in our lives that surpass our understanding and control. This acknowledgment is a humble recognition that we need God's guidance, strength, and wisdom.

Second, we're submitting our will. By asking for God's will to be done, we're essentially saying, "Here's what I think should happen in response to my requests, but I submit them to You, trusting that Your will is greater than mine."

Humble prayer is more than our words—it's the posture of our hearts.

When we remember who God is and who we are, humble prayer is the right response.

Think About It

- Do you find it hard to surrender your will to God in prayer?

- Is it possible to pray without a humble heart? What would that look like?

- Why is humility so important in the Christian life?

Pray About It

- Acknowledge who you are and who God is.

- Tell God about anything you currently need.

- Submit your will to Him.

Lord, help me always to remember what a privilege it is to be able to talk to You in prayer. Please give me a heart of gratitude and a spirit of humility.

66.
The Sinner's Prayer

And he said to Jesus, "Lord, remember me
when You come into Your holy nation."
LUKE 23:42

On the day Jesus was crucified, a thief hung on the cross beside Him. The difference between these two men? Jesus was innocent, and the thief was guilty.

The thief was being crucified for his crimes, and by the grace of God, he found himself—through no goodness of his own—in the presence of the Savior. What must have felt like the worst day of his life was actually the best, because God's mercy grabbed hold of him and changed him for eternity.

In the midst of his agony, with every breath a struggle, the thief called out to Jesus, "Lord, remember me when You come into Your holy nation." Jesus answered, "For sure, I tell you, today you will be with Me in Paradise" (Luke 23:43).

We learn so much from this simple, humble conversation. First, salvation is a matter of faith—it doesn't depend on a lifetime of good deeds or religious accomplishments. Second, humility leads to grace—the thief had no way to impress Jesus, and neither do we. Third, Jesus desires reconciliation between sinners and God—He made it possible with His death.

Have you, like the thief, humbly trusted Jesus to save you? If not, talk to God about it. If so, cherish your salvation as your greatest gift.

Think About It

- What does the story about the thief on the cross teach you about God's grace?
- How does the simplicity of the thief's faith encourage you in your own faith?
- When did you simply and humbly place your faith in Jesus to save you?

Pray About It

- Thank God for His grace.
- Thank God for including the story of the thief on the cross in the Bible.
- Talk to God about your faith in Him for salvation.

Lord, thank You for the assurance of eternal hope, made possible by the death of Jesus.

67.
The Safest Place

Trust in Him at all times, O people. Pour out your heart before Him. God is a safe place for us.
PSALM 62:8

Prayer isn't for the spiritually elite—it's for every believer. Prayer makes us all equals before God. In prayer, you don't get bonus points for being wealthy or extra merit for being good. In prayer, the saint and the seeker have the same access to conversation with God.

The safest place you could ever be is in the presence of God. The psalmist invites you to "trust in Him at all times.... Pour out your heart before Him. God is a safe place for us."

Don't make the mistake of thinking, *Someday when I'm older and wiser, I'll pray more often than I do now.* You have as much access to God today through prayer as you'll ever have in your lifetime. God is listening *now* and wants to hear from you *now.*

Whether you've been a Christian most of your life or are just starting your journey of faith, in prayer God welcomes you with open arms. In prayer, God listens to you—not because of your big achievements or your impressive words—but because He loves you as His child.

With God, you are fully known and fully safe.

Think About It

- How does the invitation to talk to God at any time impact your sense of belonging to Him?

- Do you think God wants to hear from you?

- Why do you think God wants us all to be equal before Him in prayer?

Pray About It

- Share whatever is on your heart with God.

- Ask God for courage to trust Him more.

- Tell God about anything that gets in the way of praying more faithfully.

. . . .

God, I don't want to look back on my life and realize I missed opportunities to talk to You about my days. Please help me prioritize talking to You in prayer.

68.
Just Thinking Out Loud

Keep your minds thinking about things in heaven.
Do not think about things on the earth.
COLOSSIANS 3:2

Do you ever find it hard to concentrate when you pray? You sit down and talk to God, but at some point you start thinking about everything else—what you'll wear, what you want to eat, who you need to talk to, what you have to do next. *Suddenly you realize you quit praying and didn't even notice it.*

If you've ever struggled with distraction in prayer, you aren't alone. Here are a few ideas to help you focus your mind while you talk to God:

First, if at all possible, find a quiet place to pray. The fewer distractions, the better.

Second, if you are able, kneel beside a bed, chair, or couch. Sometimes simply changing your posture can change your thoughts.

Third, pray out loud. You don't have to pray loudly or formally, but even whispering the words can help train your mind to think about what you're saying.

Finally, silence all technology—or better yet, leave your phone in another room. We may think we have the willpower to ignore notifications, but very few of us can do it successfully for very long.

God wants our hearts *and* minds engaged when we talk to Him.

Think About It

- Why is it so difficult to focus our minds in prayer?

- How can distractions hinder our connection with God in prayer?

- What is something you're willing to do in order to concentrate more effectively while praying?

Pray About It

- Talk to God about what distracts you.

- Ask God to help you focus your mind on what matters most.

- Recommit your heart and mind to Him.

God, please give me the ability to set aside the cares and distractions of this world and turn my heart totally toward You when I pray.

69.
For a Cloudy Day

Why are you sad, O my soul? Why have you become troubled within me? Hope in God, for I will praise Him again for His help of being near me.
PSALM 42:5

Let's talk about something that's not always easy to discuss but is important: despair. Despair is a profound and often overwhelming state of hopelessness, discouragement, and anguish. It's a heavy feeling, like a cloud of darkness that settles over us and makes everything seem dark and impossible. Despair can be a natural human response to devastating circumstances, but despair is not God's hope or plan for anybody's life.

David, the writer of many of our psalms, grappled with despair and often wrote about his deep sorrow and fear. One thing David clearly acknowledged in his writing: prayer is where we find hope in the midst of despair.

In addition to talking to trusted adults in your life about anything hard that you face, you should also make it a priority to talk to God. He can help. In Psalm 40:1–2 (NLT), David famously wrote, "I waited patiently for the LORD to help me, and he turned to me and heard my cry. He lifted me out of the pit of despair, out of the mud and the mire. He set my feet on solid ground and steadied me as I walked along."

God delivered David from despair. Whenever you struggle, God can deliver you too.

Think About It

- How do you think prayer contributes to hope?

- David worshipped God as a means of fighting his despair. Why do you think worship is so powerful when we're struggling or sad?

- Is it encouraging to you that David, a man after God's own heart, faced the full range of human emotion?

Pray About It

- Talk to God about anything discouraging in your life.

- Worship God—lift up His name with reverence and awe.

- Ask God to increase your hope.

....

Lord, please help me never to forget that even in despair, Your promises are steadfast and true.

70.
On Talking Terms

Never stop praying.
1 Thessalonians 5:17

First Thessalonians 5:17 is one of the best-known verses about prayer in the Bible. Many translations say, "Pray without ceasing." But what does that mean, and how is that possible?

We know God doesn't expect us to literally or physically pray all day every day, because the Bible is filled with other commands that would conflict with praying 24-7. We're supposed to faithfully attend church, joyfully give to those in need, sacrificially love our neighbors, and wholeheartedly do our work, for example. So how do we pray without stopping?

Answer: God wants us to cultivate a continuous conversation with Him.

Whether or not you own your own phone, you probably understand the idea of friends who text back and forth throughout the day. The conversation never really starts and never really ends, because they're always just picking up where they left off.

In a much greater and more important way, God wants us to keep the line of communication with Him open all the time. When you realize you need something, stop and ask for help. When you see something good or encouraging, whisper a prayer of thanks. When you sin, ask for forgiveness. Keep the conversation going. Your Creator is always ready to listen.

Think About It

- Is the idea of praying without ceasing encouraging or overwhelming to you?

- Are you good at praying short, ongoing prayers throughout your day?

- How do you think praying without ceasing could change your relationship with God?

Pray About It

- Ask God for help to pray without stopping.

- Thank God for wanting and pursuing communication with you.

- Tell God about some ordinary things happening in your life today.

....

Heavenly Father, please teach me to turn to You, not just in the big struggles, but also in the simple, mundane moments too.

71.
A Captive Audience

Whatever work you do, do it with all your heart.
Do it for the Lord and not for men.
COLOSSIANS 3:23

Prayer invites us to live for an audience of one.

Especially for teens—but really for all human beings—the idea of fitting in and keeping people happy is a big deal. Maybe you've done things you regret just to keep a crowd happy. If so, you know living your life to please everybody is exhausting and unsustainable.

In Luke 16, Jesus told His followers a parable about a dishonest manager. He concluded His story by saying, "No servant can have two bosses. He will hate the one and love the other. Or, he will be faithful to one and not faithful to the other. You cannot be faithful to God and to riches at the same time" (Luke 16:13). While Jesus was speaking specifically about the love of money, His words have a wider-reaching application. "No servant can have two bosses": You cannot be faithful to God while worshipping things like academic performance, relationships, technology, or body image.

Prayer is the way we focus our hearts on God and live for His approval alone. Through prayer, we can find the strength to break free from the pressures of people-pleasing and seek God's approval above all else.

Think About It

- Why do you think it's our tendency to seek approval from people instead of God?
- Do you think it's easier seeking God's approval or the approval of your peers?
- How might living for an audience of one change the way you live?

Pray About It

- Talk to God honestly about whether you live for His approval.
- Tell God about any temptations you have that threaten to take first place in your heart.
- Ask God for strength and courage to make Him your greatest priority.

....

God, I surrender my tendency to live for anything or anyone other than You. Today, I choose to prioritize Your approval as my audience of one.

72.
Word Up

Look through me, O God, and know my heart. Try me and know my thoughts. See if there is any sinful way in me and lead me in the way that lasts forever.

PSALM 139:23–24

One way we allow our prayers to be shaped by God's bigger purposes rather than limiting them to just our smaller, private concerns is by praying the Bible.

The Psalms are made up of text that can easily and beautifully be prayed to God with a sincere heart. For example: "Teach me Your way, O Lord. I will walk in Your truth. May my heart fear Your name" (Psalm 86:11). "Open my eyes so that I may see great things from Your Law" (Psalm 119:18). "Turn my eyes away from things that have no worth, and give me new life because of Your ways" (Psalm 119:37).

If you'd like to pray the Bible, simply read a passage (such as a psalm), reflect on whether you can honestly say the same words to God, and then—*if so*—turn the verses into a personal prayer. Use your own words or apply the verses to your life or situation.

Praying the Bible allows us to engage with it in a personal and transformative way.

Think About It

- Have you ever tried using the Bible to guide your prayers? How did that go?

- Can you think of a verse or passage that you could pray to God?

- How might praying the Bible help you grow in your relationship with God?

Pray About It

- Pray a verse to God. If you don't know where to start, use one of the verses listed in today's reading.

- In your own words, explain why the verse you chose applies to your life.

- Thank God for the gift of His Word.

....

Lord, help me to focus today on what is true, honorable, just, pure, lovely, and right (Philippians 4:8).

73.
A Fish Story

Then Jonah prayed to the Lord his God
while in the stomach of the fish.

JONAH 2:1

When we consider famous prayers in the Bible, one that probably doesn't come to mind immediately—but should—is the prayer of Jonah.

Remember, Jonah's story began with God instructing him to go to the city of Nineveh to share the gospel. But Jonah didn't want to go, so instead he boarded a ship to Tarshish, confident he could escape God's call on his life. But none of us are ever out of God's reach.

While Jonah was at sea, a terrible storm threatened to overturn the ship. Believing Jonah to be responsible for God's wrath, the sailors threw their Jewish passenger overboard.

Once in the terrible, churning waters below, Jonah was swallowed by a great big fish. This could have been the end of Jonah's story, but instead of stubbornly shaking a fist at God and dying in the creature's belly, Jonah prayed and repented of his sin. He sought God's forgiveness, and as soon as he ended his prayer, "the Lord spoke to the fish, and it spit Jonah out onto the dry land" (Jonah 2:10).

Jonah's story is a good reminder that no matter how difficult our circumstances or how persistent our sin, God is ready and willing to hear our prayer of repentance. He loves you and wants you to be right with Him.

Think About It

- When you know you've done something wrong, do you repent of your sin to God?
- What does Jonah's story teach us about repentance and mercy?
- What part does humility play in a prayer of repentance?

Pray About It

- Repent of any known sin in your heart or life.
- Ask God to protect you from sinful choices that keep you from following Him fully.
- Thank God for including Jonah's story in the Bible.

Father, help me always to be humble before You, recognizing my need for Your mercy and guidance in every aspect of my life.

74.
It's About Time

*But they who wait upon the Lord will get new strength.
They will rise up with wings like eagles. They will run
and not get tired. They will walk and not become weak.*

ISAIAH 40:31

Prayer that honors God trusts His timing.

This lesson can be hard for teens *and* adults to understand—it's a lifelong process. We live in a world where everything seems to move at hyper-speed, and waiting feels like a lost art. So when we talk to God in prayer about something that feels urgent to us but don't get the response from God we think the situation requires, it can feel like God doesn't hear us or care about what we're experiencing.

But that lie is from the devil and not from God.

We know from verses throughout the Bible that God does care. His plans for us are only and always good. So God would actually be unkind to change His will in order to match ours.

Trusting God's timing means surrendering the need for instant answers and being open to the perfect timing that He has in store for you. Trusting His timing doesn't mean sitting idly by and doing nothing while you wait, though. It means living in anticipation, knowing that God is preparing an answer for you that is far better than anything you can ask or imagine.

Think About It

- How do you think living in a world where everything is instant has impacted the way we pray?

- Can you think of a time you prayed for something and then had to wait on God to answer?

- Why is it hard to wait?

Pray About It

- Talk to God about something you are waiting on in your life.

- Express to God your trust in His timing.

- Thank God for caring about your concerns.

....

Lord, I place my trust in You, knowing that Your timing is always a reflection of Your love and care for me.

75.
Rest Assured

My soul is quiet and waits for God alone.
My hope comes from Him.
Psalm 62:5

As we've seen throughout this book, prayer is many things. It's the oxygen of the Christian life, for example, and is also a responsibility. Prayer is a declaration of dependence on God, and it's also an invitation to partner with God in the important work He's doing.

But in addition to these wonderful descriptions (among many others), prayer is also an invitation to rest.

Maybe you've never thought about prayer as rest because you aren't sleeping when you talk to God. By engaging your mind and your heart in communion with Him, you are very much awake as you pray.

Prayer offers a unique form of rest that is different from going to sleep. In prayer, we're invited to set our burdens down. Prayer is a mental and emotional break from the anxieties of this world. When we pause from our daily routines and activities in order to talk to God in prayer, that intentional break allows us to reset our hearts and minds. The act of surrendering our will to His will enables us to stop the constant striving and trust the God who has everything under control. And that is an amazing form of rest.

Think About It

- How does thinking about prayer as rest change the way you view prayer?
- How might expressing gratitude to God contribute to rest?
- Why is resting in God important?

Pray About It

- Thank God for His invitation to set your burdens down.
- Tell God why you believe He is good.
- Give God any burdens you are carrying in your life today.

....

Lord, thank You for the precious gift of being able to set my burdens down when I come to You in prayer. This is the best rest.

76.
Adding Fuel to the Fire

I can do all things because Christ gives me the strength.
PHILIPPIANS 4:13

At its core, Christian service is the way we live out our faith by actively and joyfully serving others—both in and out of our church community. We seek to love and serve others the way Jesus loved and served people when He walked on this earth. Matthew 20:28, a well-known verse, says, "For the Son of Man [Jesus' name for Himself] came not to be cared for. He came to care for others. He came to give His life so that many could be bought by His blood and made free from the punishment of sin."

Christian service is deeply influenced by the example set by Jesus, and it is fueled by faithful prayer. When you think of Christians throughout history who loved and served the church and the world well, you can be confident they did it through the power of God. Being "on fire" for Jesus isn't enough to sustain us; we need to rely on God's strength through prayer.

Living a life of Christian service in our own strength leads to burnout and limitations. However, by anchoring our service in prayer and relying on God's strength, we can persevere and make a lasting impact in the lives of others.

Think About It

- How does serving in God's strength differ from serving in your own strength?

- How do you know when you're relying on your own strength?

- Have you ever experienced burnout after trying to serve others without God's help?

Pray About It

- Talk to God about specific ways you would love to serve people someday.

- Ask God to give you His strength to obey what He commands.

- Thank God for the example of Jesus.

....

Lord, I want to serve others, so I surrender my pride and self-reliance, understanding that it is in my weakness that Your strength will be made perfect.

77.
No Easy Answers

For I hope in You, O Lord. You will answer, O Lord my God.
PSALM 38:15

We've talked about our requests. Today, let's discuss God's responses. When we pour out our honest requests before God, He responds in one of four ways.

1. He might say, "Yes." Obviously, this is the answer we most want to hear, but it's not an answer He's obligated to give. There is no magic formula for receiving the answer we want to the prayer we offer.

2. He might say, "No." This answer can be painful, and it requires us to trust the wisdom of God, believing He has our best in mind.

3. He might say, "Wait." In the waiting, we have an opportunity to be molded, refined, and prepared for whatever God has planned for the future.

4. He might say, "If." We see this answer in various stories in scripture where people prayed for mercy or intervention from God—for example, when Abraham prayed for the city of Sodom, and God said He would spare it if ten righteous people could be found there.

An "If" answer would suggest that our actions and choices play an important role in God's response.

Regardless of the answer God gives, we can be sure He hears, He cares, and He will answer us according to His good and perfect will.

Think About It

- Can you recall a time God said yes to your request?
- Can you remember a time He clearly said no to what you asked?
- Is there something you are currently waiting to hear His answer about in your life?

Pray About It

- Thank God for His willingness to hear and answer your prayers.
- Tell God about anything you don't yet understand about His responses.
- Ask God to give you more strength to trust Him in all things.

....

God, thank You for the times Your response has led me to deeper dependence on Your wisdom. Your answers are always good.

78.
In No Rush

*In the morning, O Lord, You will hear my voice. In the
morning I will lay my prayers before You and will look up.*
PSALM 5:3

Picture this scene: You're rushing through your day, juggling
your list of tasks, and your mind is a whirlwind of deadlines
and to-do lists. In the midst of your crazy, busy day, prayer is
a fleeting thought. You know you should talk to God—and
you want to talk to Him—but when? So you pray a quick
prayer for help as you run to your next class or activity.

Is that kind of prayer wrong? No, it's always good to
talk to God.

But that kind of prayer won't ultimately breathe life into
your soul. Rushing is the death of prayer.

Imagine trying to have a meaningful conversation with
someone while constantly checking your phone or looking
at your watch. It would quickly start to be a surface-level
exchange that leaves you feeling unsatisfied.

Resisting the urge to hurry and setting aside intentional
time to pray is one of the clearest ways we demonstrate to
God how much we love and value Him.

Think About It

- How would you describe the pace of your life right now? How can you make time to pray?

- What are some common obstacles that make longer prayer more difficult for you?

- How does being too busy impact your relationship with God?

Pray About It

- Talk to God about your prayer habits.

- Ask God to show you where you can make more time for Him.

- Tell God how much you love and value Him.

....

Father, I recognize the need for focused time in Your presence, where the noise of the world fades away. Please help me always to prioritize time with You.

79.
Eyes on the Prize

O Lord, I have cried to You out of the deep places. Lord,
hear my voice! Let Your ears hear the voice of my prayers.
PSALM 130:1–2

Prayer is a wonderful gift, but praying is not the end goal—
praying is a means to an end.

The goal of prayer isn't to say we've done it. If we ever find
ourselves praying just so we can feel good about having prayed,
we've missed the point. Prayer isn't the prize—relationship
with God is the prize.

So the goal of prayer is relationship with God. The psalmist wrote, "My soul waits for the Lord more than one who
watches for the morning; yes, more than one who watches for
the morning" (Psalm 130:6). This declaration doesn't sound
like someone just checking off a to-do list of spiritual disci-
plines, does it? It's much more like someone who loves God
and desperately wants to know Him better. Is Psalm 130:6
something you could genuinely say about your relationship
with your heavenly Father?

A genuine desire to connect with God is the foundation
of a meaningful prayer life. Every time we bow our heads to

pray, our goal should be to know God better and to glorify Him as a result.

Think About It

- What has been your goal in prayer?

- Do you believe consistency in prayer impacts your relationship with God? If so, how?

- How has your understanding of prayer changed since beginning this book?

Pray About It

- Tell God what your relationship with Him means to you.

- Talk to God about how you'd like to see your relationship with Him strengthened.

- Connect with God by telling Him about your day.

....

Lord, instead of empty words, I want my prayers to be a genuine expression of my desire to know You better.

80.
Disaster Zone

When I said, "My foot is going out from under me,"
Your loving-kindness held me up, O Lord. When my worry
is great within me, Your comfort brings joy to my soul.
PSALM 94:18–19

What do you do with your messy thoughts? Maybe in the quiet of your heart you wonder about the existence of God. Or maybe you've noticed hypocrisy in your church. Or maybe you struggle with the unfairness of life. What do you do when you're overwhelmed by expectations—either those set *for* you or those set *by* you?

The teenage mind can be a whirlwind of messy, sometimes scary, thoughts. These thoughts are because your brain is developing and you're thinking more deeply about issues that matter—which is good.

So what do you do when your thoughts are messy? Take them to God in prayer. Not only can God handle your messy thoughts, but He already knows them. He is more aware than you are of every jumbled, chaotic, or confusing thought that passes through your mind.

And He invites you to bring those thoughts to Him.

Think About It

- Are there any specific thoughts or topics that you find difficult to discuss with God?

- How does the realization that God already knows your messy thoughts affect your trust in Him?

- Do you ever find yourself hesitant to pray about something because you don't want to upset God? What do you think *He* would say about that?

Pray About It

- Talk to God about any messy thoughts you've been having.

- Ask God for wisdom as you continue learning to navigate life.

- Thank God for the invitation to talk to Him about anything and everything.

....

I come to You, God, not as someone who has it all figured out, but as someone who trusts that You can handle my mess.

81.
Four Golden Words

*You must have faith as you ask Him. You must
not doubt. Anyone who doubts is like a wave
which is pushed around by the sea.*

JAMES 1:6

Wouldn't it be nice if four simple words could change your life?

Good news! Here are four words that—if applied—can make a major impact: *pause and ask God.* Let's quickly unpack their meaning.

Pause. When you're faced with decisions—large or small—throughout your day, stop. How many consequences could be avoided if we learned to pause instead of acting impulsively? Pausing doesn't mean you're stuck—it proves you're wise.

Ask. Asking implies humility. It's an admission that you don't have all the answers. It's okay to have questions. There will never come a day when you have all the answers—you aren't all-knowing.

God. Asking God implies that we know *He* has the answers and will direct our steps.

When you're faced with situations throughout your day that require decisions, you will never regret pausing and asking God for wisdom.

Think About It

- How can seeking God's wisdom throughout the day positively affect your decision-making?

- Reflect on a time when you faced a major decision without seeking God's wisdom. What was the outcome?

- Do you find it challenging to pause and seek God's wisdom in your busy day?

Pray About It

- Talk to God about why it can be difficult to pause throughout the day.

- Ask God for wisdom about any choices you currently need to make.

- Praise God that He has all the answers and faithfully directs your steps.

....

Thank You, Lord, for the gift of Your wisdom that passes all understanding. Please give me the courage to pause throughout the day, draw closer to You, and trust You to guide me.

82.
Just a Reminder

"Watch and pray so that you will not be tempted. Man's spirit is willing, but the body does not have the power to do it."
MATTHEW 26:41

We don't talk frankly enough about how difficult it is to fight temptation. Our flesh, the enemy, and the world know exactly what they're doing when they place a temptation in front of us. Temptations are always tailor-made to our desires, interests, and weaknesses. They can feel like a magnetic pull, and we can almost hear them say, "Just this once won't hurt."

But sin does hurt. *Always.* Sin is never neutral in its consequences.

Yes, temptation is a force, but guess what? So is grace. When you are tempted to sin, pray and ask God to remind you what you truly want most. Do you want the short-term satisfaction that comes with sin, or do you want the long-term fulfillment that comes with pleasing God? Do you want the consequences that come with sin, or do you want the benefits of a closer relationship with the God of this universe?

Sin always looks like the better choice in a moment of temptation—but doing right is always, always, *always* the better option.

And the good news: God is ready and willing to help you when you pray.

Think About It

- Can you think of a time you fought temptation with prayer? What happened?

- Why is temptation so difficult to fight?

- Do you truly believe God wants to help you fight temptation?

Pray About It

- We all have certain temptations that are more challenging to resist. Ask God to help you fight them in His strength.

- Talk to God about what you want most.

- Thank God for His help in the battle to do what is right.

....

God, when the temptation seems overwhelming, remind me of Your presence, Your promises, and the overwhelming joy found in living a life that glorifies You.

83.
Not a Dumping Ground

If you are angry, do not let it become sin.
Get over your anger before the day is finished.
EPHESIANS 4:26

As you grow in your understanding and appreciation of prayer, here is an important point to remember: there is a fine line between praying and venting.

Have you ever caught yourself in a seemingly endless monologue with God, and you realized that it's been more of a venting session than a time of prayer? If so, you're not alone. It's easy—as we tell God about what's happening in our day—to start throwing out a list of complaints and frustrations. And pretty soon we're not really talking to God as much as we're venting and using His name to justify it.

To be clear—God wants to know *everything*. But using prayer as an excuse to complain or say whatever we want about people He created isn't prayer that honors Him.

Here are a couple of questions we should always be ready to ask ourselves as we talk to God: *Am I just venting, or am I seeking to understand God's heart for me in this situation? Do*

I just want God to make my life easier, or am I willing to be transformed in the process?

Let's be truthful in a way that honors God.

Think About It

- What do you believe distinguishes honesty from venting in prayer?

- Why do you think it's important to avoid venting and calling it prayer?

- How might venting affect your relationship with the Lord over time?

Pray About It

- Ask God to help you view people from His perspective.

- Ask God to bless those people in your life that you're currently tempted to vent about.

- Ask God to continue transforming you as you learn about prayer.

. . . .

God, please help me choose to engage in genuine and meaningful conversation with You instead of using this time as a way to vent my frustrations.

84.

The Most Important Requests You'll Ever Make

For You are good and ready to forgive, O Lord.
You are rich in loving-kindness to all who call to You.
Hear my prayer, O Lord. Listen to my cry for help.
PSALM 86:5–6

Two of the most important requests we'll ever make of God in prayer are these: *Forgive me. Help me forgive.*

First, *forgive me* stems from our awareness that we are sinful. We will break God's heart and hurt other people along the way. By seeking God's forgiveness, we humbly acknowledge our shortcomings and invite God to pour His forgiveness and mercy over us and to strengthen our relationship with Him.

Second, *help me forgive* speaks to our understanding that others will hurt us as we journey through life. This reality is painful but inevitable. Even when other people's intentions are good, they're capable of harming us. By pursuing forgiveness, we untangle the threads of resentment and bitterness that can weave knots in our hearts and build roadblocks in our relationship with God.

Forgiveness—accepting it for ourselves or offering it to others—takes courage. God will provide it if we ask.

Think About It

- Which do you find harder to do—forgive someone or ask for forgiveness?

- How does forgiving other people affect your relationship with God?

- What do you think happens when you ask God to forgive you for something?

Pray About It

- Confess that forgiving and asking for forgiveness can be uncomfortable at times.

- Ask God to help you offer and accept forgiveness when needed.

- Thank God for generously extending forgiveness to you when you ask.

. . . .

Lord, please help me to forgive others as You have forgiven me. May I extend grace to those who don't deserve it, just as Your grace has been so generously extended to me.

85.
Blessings in Disguise

In everything give thanks. This is what God
wants you to do because of Christ Jesus.
1 THESSALONIANS 5:18

Ever experience a dark day when—maybe for reasons you don't even fully understand—you feel like you're in a funk? It's like a cloud decided to camp out above your head while the sun took a vacation, and everything seems darker and more frustrating.

Grateful prayer is a remedy for difficult days.

No, not fake prayer. Not prayer that pretends everything is perfect. God already knows you're struggling on a difficult day—there's no need to pretend otherwise.

But grateful prayer can be a reset button for the heart. Grateful prayer shifts our focus from whatever is going wrong to what is still going right—from what we're missing to all we have been given. Grateful prayer says, "Maybe today isn't the best day, but there is still a lot of good in it if I'm willing to see it."

God has been so faithful, so be faithful in response.

Think About It

- Why do you think grateful prayer has the power to shift our perspective?
- Do you think it's hypocritical to offer a grateful prayer on a bad day?
- Do you believe grateful prayer glorifies God?

Pray About It

- Thank God for at least three things that you see from where you're sitting.
- Ask God to remind you about grateful prayer on your next difficult day.
- Tell God why you're grateful for Him.

. . . .

Father, thank You for small reminders that life isn't all bad, even on days when things aren't going well. On my worst days, You are still God, and You are still good.

86.
If Need Be

"Your Father knows what you need before you ask Him."
MATTHEW 6:8

As we mature in our faith and our understanding of prayer, we should learn to ask ourselves this important question: *What do I need to ask God for in this situation?*

For example. . .

Before having a difficult conversation, ask: *What do I need to ask God for in this situation?* Maybe the answer is patience, understanding, or kindness.

In the midst of difficult school assignments, ask: *What do I need to ask God for in this situation?* Maybe the answer is wisdom, perseverance, or courage to ask for help.

When facing personal insecurities, ask: *What do I need to ask God for in this situation?* Maybe the answer is trust, confidence, or a deeper understanding of your worth in Christ.

In each situation, ask the question, determine the answer, and then go to God in prayer and ask Him for that specific thing. By knowing what we need, we'll better know what to ask for in prayer. And we'll also be better able to recognize when God answers our requests.

Think About It

- How do you typically decide whether to take something you need to God or to try to solve the problem on your own?

- Are there needs you think are too big or too small for God to handle?

- Can you think of a time when you asked God to meet a specific need and He did? What did that do for your faith?

Pray About It

- Thank God for His willingness to meet your needs.

- Ask God to help you learn to ask the question *What do I need to ask God for in this situation?*

- Spend time thanking God for needs He has recently met that you haven't considered.

....

Lord, show me the beauty of learning to depend on You. Please give me greater humility to lay my needs at Your feet instead of trying to solve things on my own.

87.
Have It Both Ways

*Trust your work to the Lord, and your
plans will work out well.*

PROVERBS 16:3

Sometimes in the Christian life, we can mistakenly pit work and prayer against each other as if one makes the other unnecessary. In other words, we might fall into the trap of thinking that if we work hard, we don't really need to pray about something. Or, if we pray about something, we can just chill and let things magically fall into place.

Unfortunately, we don't find support for either of these ideas in scripture. Throughout the Bible, we see hard work and faithful prayer as an important duo.

Nehemiah prayed fervently for God to protect Jerusalem *while* actively planning and overseeing the rebuilding of Jerusalem's walls.

Paul prayed passionately for God to reach people with the gospel *while* actively writing letters and taking missionary journeys to help spread the good news.

Jesus prayed for God to forgive the sins of those who crucified Him *while* actively dying on the cross to make that forgiveness possible.

Our hard work becomes arrogant only when we use it to replace prayer and dependence on God.

Think About It

- When it comes to faithful prayer and hard work, do you find yourself leaning toward one over the other?

- Regarding prayer and work, what problems might arise if we choose to do one but not the other?

- How do you think faithfully praying and diligently working can glorify God?

Pray About It

- Talk to God about your current habits regarding faithful prayer and hard work.

- Ask God for help to do both.

- Thank the Lord for good examples in the Bible of believers who prayed and worked to the glory of God.

....

Lord, thank You for the privilege of bringing my needs before You in prayer and also working diligently for Your glory. Help me learn to do both to the best of my ability.

88.
Involve Yourself in His Plan

*But as for me, I will always have hope and
I will praise You more and more.*

Psalm 71:14

Prayer is active hope in God's goodness.

Prayer itself is the language of hope. Even if you don't know exactly what to say or you trip over your words while you pour your heart out to God, the fact that you are praying communicates hope in what you believe He is able to do.

Prayer as hope is much more than wishful thinking—it's a real affirmation of God's character. God says He is loving, holy, merciful, gracious, just, sovereign, unchanging, all-knowing, all-powerful, and all-present. By bringing your requests to God in prayer, you are confirming with your actions that you believe God is who He says He is and that you trust Him to do what He says He will do. Though we might not use these exact words, choosing to pray says, "I believe in the goodness of God, and my prayers are an expression of that belief."

So then we have to ask ourselves: *If prayer is active hope in God's goodness, what is* not praying? Not praying leads to despair.

Think About It

- How does viewing prayer as active hope expand your understanding of talking to God?

- How does praying encourage active hope in God?

- Do you typically feel more or less hopeful after you pray?

Pray About It

- Praise God for His attributes.

- Talk to Him about your hope in who He says He is and what He says He'll do.

- Ask Him to expand your hope in Him.

....

Father, please help me always to hope in You and to demonstrate that hope by faithfully talking to You in prayer.

89.
A Big Misunderstanding

We are glad for our troubles also. We know that
troubles help us learn not to give up.
ROMANS 5:3

Let's talk about the reality that some of our prayers (okay, *many* of our prayers) will not be answered the way we'd prefer.

Not getting the answers we want can be difficult and discouraging, but we can make our disappointment worse by misunderstanding what God is doing. Throughout Christian history, many people have mistakenly believed the idea that God rewards the righteous with health, wealth, and prosperity. So then, if God doesn't provide health, wealth, or prosperity, people have incorrectly assumed He's punishing them for a lack of faith.

We see no evidence in the Bible that God rewards the righteous for their faith by blessing them with health, wealth, or prosperity. In fact, we see quite the opposite. Notable examples of people with great faith who suffered include Job, Joseph, John the Baptist, many of the early Christians, and even Jesus Himself.

God, being all-knowing, sees the bigger picture and understands better than we do what we are asking. If God says no to our requests, we can assume He knows—with His perfect wisdom—that answering according to our will would not be in our ultimate best interest.

Think About It

- How can misunderstanding God's no to your prayer request hurt your faith?

- Do you think it's possible for God to love you and say no at the same time?

- How can you be sure God loves you?

Pray About It

- Talk to God about your trust in His answers to your requests.

- Ask God to strengthen your trust in Him so you can handle whatever answers He gives.

- Thank God for loving you too much to give you the wrong things.

God, I thank You that Your ways and Your thoughts are higher than my ways and my thoughts. Thank You for the times You've protected me from what I thought I wanted or needed.

90.
As Large as Life

God is able to do much more than we ask or
think through His power working in us.
EPHESIANS 3:20

Sometimes small prayers indicate small faith.

Small prayers, on their own, are not necessarily wrong or inadequate. God loves simple, sincere prayers from His children. And He doesn't want us to pray big prayers just for the sake of praying big prayers.

If our prayers are constrained by doubt, fear, or a limited perception of God's power, however, those small prayers indicate small faith. If we find ourselves consistently offering small, cautious prayers to God, we should search our hearts to see whether we truly believe God is able and willing to provide the big things that we need.

Do you have big decisions to make about your future? Do you have any complicated relationships in your life that need to be healed? Do you know friends or loved ones who still need to give their lives to Christ? Have you talked to God lately about these big requests? More to the point, do you believe God is able to answer these (and other) big requests in your life? If so, refuse to keep your prayers small.

Big prayers that demonstrate big faith bring big glory to God.

Think About It

- When was the last time you prayed and asked God for something big?

- Do you believe God is willing and able to do big things in your life?

- Do you tend to ask God for big or little things?

Pray About It

- Talk to God about any big needs or desires in your life currently.

- Tell God you want to express deeper faith and trust in Him.

- Ask God for the courage to pray prayers that glorify Him.

....

God, I know from the Bible that You parted the Red Sea and gave life to the dead and caused the walls of Jericho to fall. So please give me courage to ask and trust You for big things.

91.
All in Good Time

Rest in the Lord and be willing to wait for Him.
Do not trouble yourself when all goes well with
the one who carries out his sinful plans.

PSALM 37:7

In a world that encourages us to make impulsive decisions, praying then *waiting* on God is a countercultural discipline. Waiting on God is a refusal to give in to the pressure of just doing something ourselves or making something happen on our own. It's a refusal to act before God acts.

Imagine that a girl at school decides to gossip about you. What do you do? You could confront the girl who's gossiping. You could go to each person in her friend group and clarify your innocence. You could start some gossip about the girl who's gossiping. *Or* you could talk to God about it and wait to see what He will do.

Our current culture encourages us to hustle and to make things happen in our own strength. We're taught that if we don't do something ourselves, it won't happen at all. But God wants us to bring our requests to Him and then wait on His timing.

Is it comfortable? No. Would we rather take matters into our own hands? Often, yes. But waiting on God refines our character, deepens our trust, and strengthens our dependence on Him—all of which brings God glory.

Think About It

- Can you recall an instance when you waited on God's timing?

- How do you know when God wants you to wait on Him and not take matters into your own hands?

- Why is waiting on God uncomfortable?

Pray About It

- Talk to God about anything you are currently waiting for in your life.

- Ask God to help you learn to trust His timing.

- Ask for wisdom to know when to act and when to wait.

....

Lord, help me learn to accept the discomfort of waiting, because I know Your outcomes are better than anything I could do on my own.

92.
A Change of Heart

Jesus says yes to all of God's many promises. It is through Jesus that we say, "Let it be so," when we give thanks to God.
2 CORINTHIANS 1:20

Proverbs 19:21 says, "There are many plans in a man's heart, but it is the Lord's plan that will stand." Prayer, then, is not a negotiation with God; prayer is where we learn to surrender our plans to His will. Surrendering isn't easy. It stretches us, challenges us, and reshapes our perspective. In many ways, it requires a change of heart. That's because prayer doesn't exist to change God—prayer exists to change us!

But we are always better for surrendering to God.

The word *amen*—often used to close our prayers—is not just religious punctuation at the end of our talk to God. "Amen" is our way of communicating, "Yes, Lord. Let it be." In prayer, we have the incredible privilege of laying our needs and wants before the Lord, but ultimately the goal shouldn't be to get God to say "Amen" to what we want. Ultimately, we must learn to say "Amen" to what God decides.

Think About It

- How does understanding God's character influence your ability to surrender to His will?

- Why is it hard to surrender your will to God?

- Do you think your prayers sound more like negotiation or surrender?

Pray About It

- Boldly bring your current requests to God.

- Surrender your will to God.

- Tell God you trust that His answers to your requests will be best.

....

Lord, I surrender my plans to You, recognizing that Your ways are higher, Your understanding is deeper, and Your love is bigger than anything my limited perspective can imagine.

93.

For the Love

*"But I tell you, love those who hate you. (Respect
and give thanks for those who say bad things to you.
Do good to those who hate you.) Pray for those who do
bad things to you and who make it hard for you."*

MATTHEW 5:44

Who in your life do you struggle to love? Maybe you have
a classmate or peer who is generally unkind. Maybe one of
your friends was disloyal and broke your trust. Maybe you
have a teacher or authority figure who never seems to give
anyone the benefit of the doubt.

The Bible calls us to love even—and maybe *especially*—
when it's hard.

One way we learn to love difficult people is by remem-
bering that Jesus died for them. Since they are worth *God's*
love, who are we to say they aren't worth *our* love?

A second way we learn to love difficult people is by choosing to pray for them. God so perfectly designed our hearts
that when we genuinely pray for people we struggle to love,
we often find ourselves growing in patience, understanding,
and compassion toward them.

And think of this: sometimes the people we once struggled to love end up being deeply impactful in our lives!

Let's pray for a heart that loves deeper and wider than we ever thought possible.

Think About It

- Have you ever prayed for a difficult person in your life?

- Why does it require humility to pray that God would bless someone who is difficult to love?

- Why do you think prayer can change your heart toward someone?

Pray About It

- Pray for someone you struggle to love.

- Ask God to bless that person.

- Ask God to give you more love and patience for that person.

*Lord, please give me a heart that mirrors Yours—
one that seeks the best for others and loves unconditionally.*

94.
The Future Is Now

I am sure that God Who began the good work in you will keep on working in you until the day Jesus Christ comes again.
PHILIPPIANS 1:6

Prayer is one way we impact the future—including people we haven't yet met and events we can only imagine.

You could start praying now, for example, about a future husband, a future career, a future friend, or a future ministry. Imagine praying faithfully for something or someone for years and then having the opportunity down the road to see that something or someone and know it's a direct answer to your prayers.

Throughout history, many grandmothers have been the steadfast prayer warriors of the family tree—faithfully bringing grandchildren to God in prayer for salvation, protection, surrender, and growth. Many grandmas never get to see how God answers their requests, yet those prayers still make an impact well into the future.

For all the cultural talk about how to make a difference in the world, one of the most profound ways to impact the future is simply to close your eyes, bow your head, and pray.

Think About It

- Do you ever pray about future relationships or events in your life?

- Have you ever stopped to consider that someone in your life—maybe even long ago—may have prayed for you without your knowledge?

- Do you think God ever honors prayers for the future?

Pray About It

- Pray for something or someone in your future.

- Thank God for any people who prayed for you in the past.

- Ask God to give you a greater perspective on the power of prayer.

*Thank You, Lord, for friends and family
who bowed their heads and prayed on my behalf.
Please help me learn to do the same for others.*

95.
A Promise Kept

"If you get your life from Me and My Words live in you, ask whatever you want. It will be done for you."

JOHN 15:7

You're probably old enough to understand that life will challenge everything you say you believe. *Is God really good? Is the Bible actually true? Is the Christian life worth living?* One way we remain faithful is by reminding ourselves of the promises of God. What has God promised? He's promised salvation, guidance, peace, strength, comfort, provision, forgiveness, and hope. (And this list is just a start!)

Our prayers can help us in this fight to believe God's promises over the long haul. When we rehearse the promises of God in prayer, we don't just recite words; we deliberately ground ourselves in the unshakable truths that God has given us in His Word. Example—"Lord, in Philippians 4:19, You promised that You would supply every need according to Your riches in glory. So, God, I'm coming to You right now with a need and asking You to provide."

We honor God when we believe His promises. And there's no better place to rehearse those promises than in His presence.

Think About It

- What are three of your favorite promises of God?

- Why do you think it honors God when we believe His promises to us?

- How does talking to God about His promises give us boldness in our prayers?

Pray About It

- Talk to God about one (or more) of His promises.

- Ask God to give you the courage to believe what He said.

- Thank God for a Bible full of promises to you.

....

Lord, thank You for the unshakable truths You've included in the Bible. You didn't owe me those promises, but I'm deeply thankful for them. Help me never to take them for granted.

96.
When Praying Hurts

The Lord is near to those who have a broken heart.
And He saves those who are broken in spirit.
PSALM 34:18

If you haven't already experienced it, you will likely learn the reality that sometimes praying hurts. Sometimes it hurts because we've prayed for something sincerely and faithfully and God hasn't said yes. Sometimes prayer hurts because our hearts have been broken by the messiness of life and we don't know what to say when we come to God in prayer. Sometimes it hurts because of our own regrettable choices or harmful decisions.

Praying without ceasing requires that we pray every day, including the worst days of our lives—and that could mean we pray while our hearts are breaking.

Pray anyway. It's okay to talk to God with your heart in pieces and tears streaming down your face. In fact, God is always the right one to talk to when you're suffering.

Be honest. With whatever words you can muster, tell God the truth. "God, this situation hurts. I don't understand, and I need You to fix this mess."

Trust Him. In the midst of your hurt, God sees you, hears you, and holds you in the palm of His hand.

Think About It

- Have you ever experienced a day when praying was painful?

- Is it easier or harder for you to pray when your heart is broken? Why?

- What do you do when you don't know what to say to God?

Pray About It

- Talk to God about any current difficulties or disappointments in your life.

- Tell God your desire to keep showing up on difficult days.

- Ask God to give you courage to trust Him fully.

....

Lord, help me always to be willing to bring You the hurts that I carry and the wounds too deep to express. Whether it's the pain of a broken heart, the weight of unanswered questions, or the ache of healing that hasn't happened, help me to trust You with it.

97

The Church Underground

We do not look at the things that can be seen. We look at the things that cannot be seen. The things that can be seen will come to an end. But the things that cannot be seen will last forever.
2 CORINTHIANS 4:18

Have you ever wished you could do something to help Christians who are being persecuted for their faith? You can pray.

Every day, millions of Christians around the world face abuse, oppression, mistreatment, and even death for their faith. As Christians, we *should* remember our brothers and sisters in Christ who face persecution. But what do we pray?

Here are a few ideas to get you started. Pray that they would rely on God and not themselves, that they would continue telling others about Jesus, that their witness would impact those who try to harm them, that they would experience the overwhelming peace of God in their suffering, that they would be protected, and that they would sense the nearness of God at all times.

We know God cares deeply for His church and loves each child He calls His own. So when we pray for the persecuted church, we're aligning our hearts to His and He hears us.

Think About It

- Do you pray for the persecuted church?

- Do you believe prayer for persecuted believers makes a difference? Why or why not?

- In addition to the list in today's reading, what are two additional requests you can pray on behalf of the persecuted church?

Pray About It

- Pray for fellow believers who are suffering around the world for their faith.

- Ask God to protect and provide for Christians living in countries where the Christian faith is illegal.

- Ask God for a deeper appreciation of the religious freedoms you have where you live.

....

Lord, in addition to praying for brothers and sisters being persecuted for their faith, I pray for those doing the harm. Please soften their hearts and open their eyes to the truth of the gospel.

98.
When You Least Expect It

*Dear friends, let us continue to love one another,
for love comes from God. Anyone who loves is a
child of God and knows God. But anyone who does
not love does not know God, for God is love.*

1 JOHN 4:7–8 NLT

By now, you understand that prayer is far less about the answers and far more about the Answerer.

That's the beauty of prayer over time. When we first start out praying, we bring a list of things we want. Some of the items on our list are eternally important, but most of them probably aren't. Over time—as we faithfully meet with God—we begin to better understand that prayer isn't about a transaction—it's about our transformation. We are the ones who are changing day by day.

The more we learn the heart of God, the more we lay down our plans and embrace His. We start to see our circumstances through His eyes. We find true and lasting joy in His presence, even when the answers we seek don't unfold the way we imagined. Through faithful prayer, we learn to love God and His plans for our lives.

And then one day when we least expect it, we realize we don't really need the answers from God that we originally thought. We find that *He* has become the ultimate answer to our deepest longings.

Think About It

- How has your understanding of prayer changed or grown while reading this book?

- What goals do you have for your life of prayer with God?

- What do you believe is the key to loving God and His plans for your life?

Pray About It

- Thank God for the good gift of prayer.

- Ask God to continue growing your love for Him.

- Tell God what you hope your prayer life will look like one year from now.

Thank You, Lord, for Your extraordinary gift of prayer.

99.
Stop at Nothing

You do not get things because you do not ask for them.
JAMES 4:2

Some final words for when you close this book and continue pursuing a life of prayer with God: *you'll never get an answer to a prayer you don't pray.*

Maybe you don't know if you have enough time to pray; maybe you're afraid to bring your requests to God; maybe you're not really sure how prayer works and you still have questions. *Or maybe* you're nervous that God won't answer your prayer in the way that you desire. But if you don't ask, you definitely won't get the answer you hope to receive!

So keep praying. Even without the perfect prayer routine or the right words for every prayer, keep inviting God into your everyday moments. Talk to God often and honestly. Tell Him anything and everything.

Whatever holds you back from talking to God in prayer will hold you back from the blessings God has for you in your relationship with Him. So whether you're on cloud nine or knee-deep in a messy life situation, just show up. Keep talking to Him. Keep learning from Him. Keep trusting Him. You never know what God will do with your prayer when you offer it with a sincere heart.

Think About It

- Are you willing to keep praying when life gets hard?
- Is anything currently holding you back from faithful prayer?
- What is one more goal you have for your life of prayer?

Pray About It

- Ask God to help you stay faithful in prayer.
- Talk to God about any concerns that hold you back.
- Ask God to remind you to talk to Him throughout the day.

....

Lord, help my prayers to be not empty words but expressions of a genuine heart surrendered to Your will.

100.
The Beginning

I pray that you will know the love of Christ.
His love goes beyond anything we can understand.
I pray that you will be filled with God Himself.
EPHESIANS 3:19

Don't think of this as the end of your journey—think of it as your first step into a new one with all the new information you've learned about prayer. Once you learn to love prayer and communication with God, the sky is literally the limit.

Nothing is sweeter than loving and being loved by God.

And now a prayer *for* you, taken from the apostle Paul's prayer for the church: "I pray that you will be able to understand how wide and how long and how high and how deep His love is. I pray that you will know the love of Christ. His love goes beyond anything we can understand. I pray that you will be filled with God Himself. God is able to do much more than we ask or think through His power working in us. May we see His shining-greatness in the church. May all people in all time honor Christ Jesus. Let it be so" (Ephesians 3:18–21).

Walk with God. The journey just keeps getting better.

Think About It

- What do you want to learn next about God and His Word?

- What do you hope to keep learning about prayer?

- How will you use what you've learned so far to strengthen your faith?

Pray About It

- Admit you're still seeking answers to tough questions.

- Invite God to teach you more about Himself and His Word.

- Thank Him for the honor of prayer.

....

Every day, I have new questions, Lord. And every day, You have answers for me in Your Word. Thank You for this journey in prayer. Help me to never stop walking toward You.

Also for Teen Girls

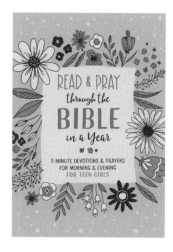

This delightful devotional, created especially for teen girls like you, features a simple plan for reading and praying through the Bible in one year alongside a 3-minute devotional reading for the morning and a 3-minute prayer for the evening. Each day's readings provide practical spiritual takeaways for everyday living.

Paperback / ISBN 978-1-63609-068-9